Love

Blackwell Brief Histories of Religion Series

This series offers brief, accessible, and lively accounts of key topics within theology and religion. Each volume presents both academic and general readers with a selected history of topics which have had a profound effect on religious and cultural life. The word "history" is, therefore, understood in its broadest cultural and social sense. The volumes are based on serious scholarship but they are written engagingly and in terms readily understood by general readers.

Published

Heaven	Alister E. McGrath
Heresy	G. R. Evans
Islam	Tamara Sonn
Death	Douglas J. Davies
Saints	Lawrence S. Cunningham
Christianity	Carter Lindberg
Dante	Peter S. Hawkins
Spirituality	Philip Sheldrake
Cults and New Religions	Douglas E. Cowan and David G. Bromley
Love	Carter Lindberg

Forthcoming

Judaism	Steven L. Jacobs
Reformation	Kenneth Appold
Eastern Christianity	Ailyne Smith

Love

A Brief History Through Western Christianity

Carter Lindberg

Blackwell
Publishing

BV
4639
.L495
2008

BLACKWELL PUBLISHING
350 Main Street, Malden, MA 02148-5020, USA
9600 Garsington Road, Oxford OX4 2DQ, UK
550 Swanston Street, Carlton, Victoria 3053, Australia

First published 2008 by Blackwell Publishing Ltd

1   2008

Library of Congress Cataloging-in-Publication Data

Lindberg, Carter, 1937–
    Love : a brief history through Western Christianity / Carter Lindberg.
      p. cm.—(Blackwell brief histories of religion series)
    Includes bibliographical references and index.
    ISBN 978-0-631-23598-9 (hardcover : alk. paper)—ISBN 978-0-631-23599-6 (pbk. : alk. paper) 1. Love—Religious aspects—Christianity. I. Title.

    BV4639.L495 2008
    241'.4—dc22

                                    2007041657

A catalogue record for this title is available from the British Library.

Set in 10/12.5pt Meridian
by SPi Publisher Services Pondicherry, India
Printed and bound in Singapore
by Fabulous Printers Pte Ltd

The publisher's policy is to use permanent paper from mills that operate a sustainable forestry policy, and which has been manufactured from pulp processed using acid-free and elementary chlorine-free practices. Furthermore, the publisher ensures that the text paper and cover board used have met acceptable environmental accreditation standards.

For further information on
Blackwell Publishing, visit our website at
www.blackwellpublishing.com

To Alice

Contents

Preface

"What is sweeter than honey? What is stronger than a lion?"
Judges 14:18

For Samson, that great athlete, sexual and otherwise, whose story is related in the book of Judges, the answer to the riddle is love. As the story progresses through Samson's affair with Delilah, we learn that love not only makes the world go 'round; lack of love literally brings everything crashing down. In the words of the Song of Songs (8:6–7): "love is strong as death, passion as fierce as the grave. Its flashes are flashes of fire, a raging flame. Many waters cannot quench love, neither can floods drown it." The centrality of love to human life permeates biblical writings from the erotic poetry of the Song of Songs to the shorthand gospel of John 3:16 that "God so loved the world that he gave his only Son, so that everyone who believes in him may not perish but may have eternal life." Not only the biblical writers, but philosophers, poets, and theologians from Plato through Dante to C. S. Lewis have struggled to describe, define, and demonstrate love. Their efforts continue to inform, deform, and reform present understandings and experiences of love. The history of love ranges from Adam and Eve to the most recent pot-boiler romance novel, from star-crossed lovers to parents and children, from friends to enemies, from medieval troubadours to contemporary minstrels of all stripes, from churches to talk shows. Is love an "eternal idea"? Or does the understanding of love have a history? Does love change, grow, diminish? Does spousal profession of love have the same meaning at the altar and at the golden anniversary? Can marriage be based on love? Is love in an arranged marriage of the tenth century comparable to love in a voluntary marriage of the twenty-first? Indeed, what do marriage and love have to do with each other? Do parents love their children less or more now than in prior times? Is love a feeling? Is love an act? Is love an art? Is love voluntary or involuntary, or both? How is self-love related to love of the neighbor? Does love extend to enemies? What is the relation of love to sexuality? Can love be commanded? Is love redemptive? Is love divine? Is divinity love? How does love form and inform our existence? What, indeed, *is* love? The questions seem to have no end, and any effort to set forth a history of love, especially a "brief" one, must be highly selective. Rather than "justify" my selections, I take refuge in the candor of Eusebius (c.260–c.340), "the father of church history," who wrote at the beginning of his *The History of the Church*: "I have picked out whatever seems relevant to the task I have undertaken, plucking like flowers in literary pastures the helpful contributions of earlier writers, to be embodied in the continuous narrative I have in mind." Obviously, in the following "history," many beautiful flowers have been left in the pastures.

The following "brief history of love" presents some of the theoretical and practical "answers" to questions about love set forth in Western culture from early reflections in

Greco-Roman culture to the present. Since a dominant thread running through Western culture is Christianity in its many expressions, we shall approach our subject from its perspective. But even this limitation is too broad because every aspect of Christian theology expresses in one way or another a concept of love. It is possible under the rubric of love to include anything and everything. Library shelves groan under the weight of innumerable studies on this theme. To read and understand even a small fraction of all these studies is far beyond my ability. There is also the dangerous professorial penchant of killing the subject. As Søren Kierkegaard noted, theology professors too often reverse the miracle of Cana: they turn wine into water. Therefore I have attempted a broad narrative of love in Western history. The downside of such a ''brief'' history is that every reader will miss his or her favorite philosopher, theologian, or saint. I hope that in spite of such disappointments, this little volume may provide an entrée to a fascinating and complex subject. To that end, I have avoided footnotes but have provided a bibliography of the works directly informing my views for those who wish to fill in the gaps of this endeavor as well as find correctives to my synthesis.

So many people have contributed to this project that there is not space to grant them their deserved gratitude. Blackwell's editors, especially Rebecca Harkin, have been wonderfully supportive. I am grateful to students at Boston University School of Theology who shared their insights in seminars on the topic of Christian love. I am also grateful to the Lutheran Theological Seminary at Philadelphia where I was privileged to be the St. John's Visiting Professor of Church History in the spring of 2005. The students there in the seminar on Christian love provided valuable insights and perspectives, but of course like my other students should not be blamed for the final text. Our neighbors, Pat and Deb Garner, often – with wine-fortified courage! – asked how this project was going, listened patiently, and asked great questions during the many months of writing. As always I am grateful to George W. Forell, my Doktor-Vater, perpetual mentor, and friend, who many decades ago introduced me to this subject in his own seminar, and then guided my dissertation on Luther's concept of love. Above all, I am grateful for the love and laughter of Alice.

Chapter 1

The Language of Love

"The Greeks have a word for it" is an old cliché but nonetheless apt for our subject. Indeed, in relation to "love," the Greeks not only had *a* word, they had many words! Like so many aspects of Western culture, our understandings and views of love have been influenced by contributions from Greek thought. The Greek vocabulary for "love" includes the nouns "storge," "epithymia," "philia," "eros," and "agape," and their respective verb forms. On occasion some of these words for love are interchangeable but they are not strong synonyms. As we shall see, the history of the language of love is intimately related to the history of ideas. But as some wag once put it, the history of ideas is akin to nailing jello to the wall. Hence, caveat emptor, readers are warned that past historical contexts are often foreign countries and that words familiar to us may have been used quite differently in different times and places. For example, Cheyette notes in his study of medieval troubadour literature that when we moderns limit our concept of love to a sentiment, we miss its medieval political and social meanings. Bolkestein makes a similar point in his study of pre-Christian social welfare when he notes that in classical culture "philanthropy" meant love among men or human love not charity or social welfare. And Jaeger notes that by the time of Shakespeare, the increasing privatization of love viewed public expressions of love for such charismatic persons as kings, rulers, churchmen, and saints – common in the Middle Ages – as hypocritical gambits for advancement.

Some of the many Greek terms for love no longer have much currency in our vocabulary. *Storge*, a more literary term for familial love or parental affection, and *epithymia*, a term associated with libido or desire have not had a significant impact on the Western vocabulary of love. *Philia*, *eros*, and *agape*, on the other hand, have significantly influenced Western languages and ideas. *Philia*, with meanings of friendship, close family relations, and human solidarity, is familiar in its English forms of *philadelphia* for brotherly love and philanthropy for benevolence. These expressions of concern for the well-being of others, both of which are present in the Greek New Testament, are reversed in the related term philander. Eros is familiar in modern languages in the related forms of the word "erotic."

In the pre-philosophical Greek cosmogonies, theories of the generation or birth of the cosmos, Eros appears as a uniting force. Hesiod, the great eighth-century-BCE poet next to Homer, presents Eros as one of the first to emerge from the dark abyss of Chaos, and then as the one who draws everything together, the creative, uniting force. Eros is "the most beautiful of the immortal gods, who in every man and every god softens the sinews and overpowers the prudent purpose of the mind." Ancient Greek literature portrays Eros as a violent, crafty god whose arrows drive people into torment and passion for the first person seen after they are struck. In the later Greek myths, Eros is the personification of love as sexual desire.

His famous shrine at Thespiai, a site for Plutarch's (45–c.125 CE) *Erotikos* ("Dialogue on Love"), held quadrennial festivals to love. Eros was often presented as the son of Aphrodite (Venus to the Romans; goddess of love and beauty) and Ares (Mars to the Romans; god of war). Hesiod portrays Aphrodite's origin in the white foam that arose from the severed genitals of Uranus thrown in the sea by his son Cronos. Hence the famous Botticelli image of Venus on the half-shell arising from the sea. And Ares, Homer tells us in the *Iliad*, was hated by his father Zeus. With parents like that, it is no wonder that Western culture has perennially associated sex and violence. Epicurus (300 BCE) defined Eros as "a strong appetite for sexual pleasures, accompanied by furor and agony." The aggressive aspect of love in the Greek tradition often portrayed the lover as pursuer. Thus in the myth of Apollo and Daphne, Apollo – the god of manly youth and beauty – pursued the nymph Daphne who escaped him by being transformed into a Laurel tree. One needs only to review the Greek myths to realize that Freud was not the first to posit the relationship of sex and death, nor was Stanley Kubrick's 1964 movie, *Dr. Strangelove or How I Learned to Stop Worrying and Love the Bomb*, its first artistic expression.

Eros, the handsome god of sexual love – "the most beautiful of all the gods" – also is associated with the chaos and death accompanying the violent physical desire seen in the stories of Paris and Helen, Zeus and Hera. Paris gave the "apple of discord," a gold apple inscribed "for the fairest," to Aphrodite who thereupon promised him the most beautiful woman in the world, Helen. So Paris carried off Helen, the wife of Menelaus, thereby setting in motion the Trojan War, the destruction of Troy, the death of Achilles, and his own death. The Olympian gods, of whom Zeus is the "father," were not paragons of monogamous or faithful marriages, but rather it seems the initiators and models of the dysfunctional family. Their love stories are stories of violence and rape. The relations of Zeus and his sister-wife Hera with each other as well as others cannot be abbreviated here, but their activities in sex and war make the most bizarre television talk shows pale in comparison. The Greek poets could portray Eros as cunning and cruel, instilling people with a maniacal drive that disrupts reason and life itself, a theme later explored in Plato's (c.429–327 BCE) *Phaedrus*. Centuries after Hesiod, the Roman poet Ovid (43 BCE–17 CE) noted in his *The Art of Love*, "love is a kind of war." We often forget this disruptive element because we are more familiar with the personification of Eros under his Latin name, Cupid (also named Amor). But the cute, winged, chubby lad of our Valentine's Day cards is far removed from the primal force of nature with its potential for mad passion, the irrationality and chaos epitomized by Eros's sharp arrows that cause severe, painful, and even mortal wounds. There is a sense in which this divine madness of Eros was "baptized" in medieval and early modern Catholic mysticism. For example, St. Teresa of Avila (1515–1582), a "Doctor of the Church" since 1970, wrote of the divine madness that overcame her when pierced by the arrows of God her Lover: "The pain was so great that I screamed aloud; but at the same time I felt such infinite sweetness that I wished the pain to last forever." The (orgasmic) rapture of such wounds are captured in Bernini's sculpture "The Ecstasy of St. Teresa" (1645–1652; Santa Maria Vittoria, Rome) that depicts her "transverberation" – an angel plunging a flaming golden arrow into her heart. When the angel withdrew the arrow, "I thought he was carrying off with him the deepest part of me; and he left me all on fire with great love of God." The image is repeated in the baroque engraving, "Beatrice and the Arrow of Divine Love" (by Liska, 1708) that depicts the Cistercian Beatrice of Nazareth (1200–1268) being stabbed in the chest by an arrow.

A classic Greek expression of the effort to exert rational control over Eros or at least to gain understanding of such love is Plato's dialogue *Symposium*, also known as the *Banquet*. Martha Nussbaum in her study, *The Fragility of Goodness*, extensively analyses the historical–political context and multi-faceted content of this dialogue, juxtaposing Socrates' famous speech on love (Eros) to that of Alcibiades. I shall focus on Socrates to the neglect of the other major participants because it is largely Socrates' perspective that has influenced the idea of love as an ascent from the material to the spiritual world, the striving for immortality. The immediate setting for the dialogue is a banquet hosted by the poet Agathon who has just won a prize for his poetry. The company decides that their topic of conversation will be Eros. When it is Socrates' turn to discuss love, he relates the knowledge of love revealed to him by the priestess Diotima. Love is either the desire for that which is not possessed or the desire not to lose what is loved. In either case, love is marked by a lack and thus the desire to acquire what is lacking. This is because, Diotima explains, love was born at the gods' feast celebrating Aphrodite's birthday at which Poverty and the god Plenty slept together and conceived Love, who is neither mortal nor immortal. In Diotima's words, love "is always poor," "is always in distress," always in search of fulfillment. Here Eros is the human quest for fulfillment; the drive to possess the good forever.

Plato's understanding of love is tied to his *eudaimonia* (eudaemonism), often translated as the drive toward happiness. We miss the dynamic of eudaemonism, however, if we think of it in a modern psychological sense of feeling pleasure. Plato, and then Aristotle, thought of eudaemonism as an active drive (*daimon*) toward the good (*eu*), that is, the drive to living and doing well. Diotima says to Socrates: "the happy are made happy by the acquisition of good things." Eros in this sense is what C.S. Lewis in *The Four Loves* termed "need-love." Love is the striving or ambition that characterizes all human activity. However, the love of pleasure, wealth, fame, persons, beauty does not finally alleviate love's poverty or need because all temporal things perish. That is why, Diotima affirms, "all men . . . desire the immortal." Ascent toward immortality begins on the biological level – the hope that children will preserve the memory of the father – and progresses toward the more permanent "children" of fame and ideas. "Who," Diotima says, "when he thinks of Homer and Hesiod and other great poets, would not rather have their children than ordinary human ones?" The imagery of ascent is explicit: "[B]egin from the beauties of the earth and mount upward for the sake of that other beauty, using these as steps only, and from one going on to two, and from two to all fair forms, and from fair forms to fair practices, and from fair practices to fair notions, until from fair notions . . . [to] the notion of absolute beauty, . . ." The perception of beauty in the world recalls in the soul the memory of ideal beauty, and the recollection of beauty and truth inspire yearning for a higher existence in the realm of pure ideas; an immortal realm not subject to the decay and death of the world. With its spiritualizing ascent to the primal form of beauty, the soul discovers a radiance of the Beautiful, the inspired order of the world. The motif of ascent from lower to higher, earth to heaven, will imbue medieval Christian mysticism and theology. The influence of Plato's *Symposium* extended into the early modern period through Dante's (1265–1321) *Convivio* and Marsilio Ficino's (1433–1499) *Commentary on Plato's Symposium on Love* that in turn influenced literature for the next couple of centuries.

The downside of this Hellenistic "beatific vision" was that in identifying the good with the beautiful, there arose the tendency to associate evil with the ugly and the deformed. As Younger notes in the entry "Beauty Contests" in his *Sex in the Ancient World*, "male beauty was considered to connote good character. Similarly, the ugly man was reckoned poor in spirit. . . ." It should be added that the Greeks were not alone in associating external circumstances of life with the intellectual, spiritual, and moral condition of persons. In the Bible, Job's sufferings are attributed to his sin; in the medieval period, leprosy is seen as a disease of the soul, and the Knights of the Round Table are always exceedingly handsome; in our days, poverty is often attributed to a moral flaw in the poor person.

The image of love as an ascent motivated by a hierarchy of increasing value for the lover is graphically displayed in the long art history of images of the ladder to heaven. The best known of these innumerable artistic renditions relate, in the Byzantine world, to John Climacus's (c.570–c.649) "Ladder of Paradise" and in the medieval West to the "Ladder of Virtues" in the twelfth-century "Garden of Delights." In the Garden of Delights image, figures fall off the ladder because they are attracted to lesser goods than the highest good, heaven, at the top of the ladder. It is significant that the figure at the very top of the ladder receiving the "crown of life" from the hand of God is labeled "caritas," medieval Latin for love. Thus Plato's recasting of the older myths of Eros into a teleology of love was appropriated by Christian iconography. Love is directed toward an end, toward an immortality freed from the fetters of physical existence, freed from the downward pull of appetites such as sexual desire, and freed from loving things or persons for their own sake because eternal happiness cannot be acquired in what is perishable. Eros is finally the desire to overcome desire. Paradoxically, then, Eros may lead to asceticism. At any rate, Eros is the ladder to divinity, from the perishable world to the imperishable, from mortality to immortality. So understood, love is redemptive; it transcends the vulnerabilities of life in the world. Yet in a sense this may be called a kind of redemptive hedonism, the search for spiritual pleasure beyond mere physical pleasure; the use of things and others for one's quest for immortality. That is why some have argued that Platonic Eros is ultimately egocentric, self-love desiring to be self-sufficient.

Although Aristotle (384–322 BCE) differed significantly from his teacher Plato in ways we cannot pursue here, he too conceived of love as an ascent or a striving for perfection, for pure form in Aristotle's terms. Aristotle rationalized the ancient Greek Eros into the "Unmoved Mover." In Aristotle's chapter on the "Eternal Being" in his *Metaphysics* he concludes: "The self-sufficient activity of the divine is life at its eternal best. We maintain, therefore, that the divine is the eternal best living being, so that the divine is life unending, continuous, and eternal. . . . It has also been shown that the first mover cannot be moved [because it is without attributes; it is impassive] and is unalterable. . . . " The Unmoved Mover moves us "as an object of love." As Pure Form, it does not itself act but rather its perfection kindles eros to strive for it. The world and all its life arises from its longing for God. Thus, love is a one-way street: humankind must love God; but it is impossible for God to love humankind for that would detract from the perfection of the First Cause which cannot think of anything except what is perfect, i.e., himself.

In the eighth and ninth books of his *Nicomachean Ethics*, Aristotle also diverges from Plato in discussing friendship as a love of benevolence rather than a love of desire. Thus the guiding conceptual word is not eros but *philia*. Nussbaum argues that "friendship" is too weak a translation of *philia* because it does not convey the "very strongest affective relationships that human beings form," including those that have a "passionate sexual component." She prefers to translate *philia* by the word "love." Bolkestein also notes that "friendship" is not identical with the Greek "philia," a word that includes affective relations closer to what moderns term love, such as those of parents and children, brothers and sisters. *Philia* also has the meanings of comradeship and social affiliations. In Aristotle's *Ethics*, he placed *philia* in his doctrine of the practical virtues. *Philia* as a feeling rests upon a *habitus* ("habit" in the sense of a characteristic attained by repeated, habitual action). The one loving in the sense of *philia* therefore wills the good differently than the person moved by erotic desire: he wills the good for the other for the sake of the other. The lovable is of three forms: the good, the pleasurable, and the useful. Correspondingly there are three forms of friendship. The consummate friendship is that of the good. In this friendship the friend is loved for his or her own sake, not for the sake of something useful or pleasurable that is obtainable through him or her. Their friendship is durable, based upon trust and mutuality.

This friendship-love grounded upon willing the good for the other for the sake of the other is named *eunoia*, benevolence. Because rationally one always desires the good for oneself, the question remains about the possibility of benevolent relationships. Aristotle answers that love to another derives from self-love (*philautia*). The precedence of self-love has its source in a universal principle. All existing being is affirmable and lovable being. Thus when a master craftsman loves his work, he fundamentally loves himself, i.e., his own self, becoming manifest in the work; a similar transference illustrates love to others, to friends. Thus each person initially loves himself, and each person is himself his best friend. To love means to assign good things to the beloved. The self-love that thinks the good exists in possessions, honor, and bodily pleasure is reprehensible. True self-love allots oneself the most beautiful and the good in the highest sense; in this way the person lives to please the best in him or herself. Hence, in this self-love there is also the possibility of self-sacrifice. Still even if a person renounces a noble deed for his friend, he acts according to the command of self-love: with his magnanimous renunciation he allocates to himself the better lot. "[I]f all men were to compete for what is noble and put all their efforts into the performance of the noblest actions, all the needs of the community will have been met, and each individual will have the greatest of goods, since that is what virtue is." The Aristotelian orientation to friendship was continued by Cicero (106–43 BCE).

Cicero's writing on friendship, *De amicitia*, was appropriated by medieval Christian culture and blended with biblical precepts by, among others, the famous Cistercian abbot and spiritual writer, Aelred of Rievaulx (1110–1167), the "patron saint of friendship." Some scholars have suggested that Aelred's best known work, *Spiritual Friendship*, is mainly a reworking of Cicero's *De amicitia*. Another example is Richard de Fournival (1201–1260), physician and cleric, whose *Advice on Love* praises love as "the virtue of virtues." Thus, "as Cicero tells us, self-interest must come second to love, not vice-versa." Fournival refers to Cicero's oft-repeated definition of friendship when he writes: "Cicero is speaking about such spiritual love when he says that love is a common feeling of compassion and good will for all things divine and human."

It was the Roman poet Virgil (70–19 BCE) who gave Western culture one of its most overworked phrases: "Amor vincit omnia." "Love conquers all" – the inscription on Chaucer's Prioress's brooch – is so commonplace that its origin in Virgil's *Eclogue* is often forgotten. His epic *Aeneid* on the foundation of Rome, as well as his other writings, were a staple of Western Christian culture through the Renaissance, and he was believed to be a "Christian by nature" before Christ because of his ethics. Virgil is Dante's guide through Hell and Purgatory, but has to remain in Limbo.

In addition to the classical influences of Plato, Aristotle, and Cicero, the works of Plutarch (45–c.125 CE) and Ovid have been interwoven in Western concepts of love up to the present. Plutarch's celebration and promulgation of the philosophy and values of Greece, whose political viability by his time had been replaced by Rome, find expression in his *Moralia*. Among these collected essays on ethics are treatises on love, brotherly love, and marriage, as well as on friendship and the education of children; writings admired by Montaigne and Shakespeare. Plutarch softened the sharp edges of the received Platonic misogyny in discussing marriage as companionship and friendship. Physical intimacies in marriage, he wrote, "are the seeds of friendship;" and it is absurd "to declare that women have no share in excellence." We are to honor and cultivate friends and relatives "for we are neither able nor by nature fitted to live solitary, without friends and without companionship."

Plutarch's dialogue on "Love" (*Erotikos*), an echo of Plato's *Symposium*, is of interest for his praise of marriage over "boy-love." It seems that pederasty may still have been a matter of debate centuries after the late Plato began to question it and Aristotle had condemned homosexual relationships as a disease. In *Erotikos*, Protogenes claims that "there is only one genuine Love, that of boys," and that "of true Love the women's apartment has no shred." The only reason for marriage is that it is "necessary for the propagation of the race." In response, Daphnaios asserts that marriage leads to friendship and mutual respect whereas boy-love is contrary to nature. "But the love of virtuous women not only undergoes no autumn, but flourishes even with hoary head and wrinkles and abides forever in tombs and monuments. Very few unions of male lovers have endured, but of men and women joined in love we can count myriads of cases where unions wholly faithful have been maintained loyally and eagerly to the end." The dialogue, including other participants, reviews the classical Hellenistic views and stories of Eros including the sense of divinely inspired "madness." "This passion is commonly called 'enthusiasm,' . . . because it shares and participates in a divine [*theos*] power." "Enthusiasm" is literally "God-withinism" (*entheos*).

One of the most influential classical writers upon medieval literature and the development of what is known today as "courtly love" was Ovid. He is best known for his *Ars amatoria* (*The Art of Love*) and *Amoris remedia* (*Cures for Love*). These two works in particular are clear sources for Andreas Capellanus's (twelfth-century) *De arte honesti amandi*, usually called *The Art of Courtly Love*, and for the *Roman de la Rose* (*The Romance of the Rose*) (thirteenth century) begun by Guillaume de Lorris and completed by Jean de Meun. As Allen notes, the major French writers of the eleventh century knew Ovid as well as the Bible by heart. However, all too often, medieval writers did not grasp Ovid's parody and satire, and thus took him seriously. Francesco Petrarch (1304–1374) thought Ovid wanton and condemned his *Ars amatoria*. On the other hand, Giovanni Boccaccio (1313–1375) praised Ovid for showing how "to kindle the sacred fires of Venus in cold hearts," and used his stories in the *Decameron*. And Chaucer (1343–1400) referred to Ovid as "Venus's clerk."

As mentioned earlier, Ovid compared love to war: "Love is a kind of war, and no assignment for cowards;" and every lover is a warrior under the command of Love. Ovid's advice when caught in multiple affairs: "swear up and down it's a lie. . . . Wear yourself out if you must, and prove, in her bed, that you could not possibly be that good, coming from some other girl." Indeed, affairs should be kept secret to avoid the complications that arise from angry husbands and jealous women. Ovid adds that this very secrecy will make affairs more pleasant. Deceit and manipulation are among the techniques the teacher in this manual of seduction promotes as skills the reader may practice to gain his goal.

With the rise of Christianity as a world religion, the classical reflections on love were called into question by the church. The initial critique from the side of the biblical tradition was not primarily ethical but rather theological. The biblical tradition was totally at odds with the common Greek conviction that the relationship of the gods to humankind excludes a love relationship. As noted, Aristotle thematized love cosmologically with his argument of the unmoved mover. In his *Metaphysics*, Aristotle posited the highest good as the ultimate ground of movement because it moves others as the object of their love and desire. The Absolute is the quintessence of perfection that thereby moves everything to strive for it. The final cause thereby remains in itself exempt from movement because movement denotes a lack, a desire for fulfillment. Since the Absolute lacks nothing it also desires nothing. Thus the Absolute need not and does not communicate with any but the Absolute. In his *Nicomachean Ethics*, love in the form of self-love becomes relevant as it moves the virtuous to implement for himself the most beautiful and best actions.

Between the Platonic theory of Eros and the Aristotelian teaching of friendly benevolence on the one side and the beginnings of a Christian theology on the other side there appeared at first to be an unbridgeable gap. The Bible understands the relationship between God and the people of Israel and thus extending to humankind to be a relationship of reciprocal love; a relationship that therefore includes self-disclosure and communication. In the Bible, God is presented as the God who communicates his own self to humankind. Furthermore, the Hellenistic anthropocentric perspective permeated the "divine Eros" making it – in its better expressions! – analogous to human love. The biblical perspective viewed human love from a theocentric perspective – love to others is to be analogous to divine love. In contrast to Aristotle's Unmoved Mover, the biblical God enters history, moves and loves humankind encouraging people to call him "Abba," i.e., "Father." To say "our Father" expresses a relationship of trustful love.

Furthermore, "love" in the biblical accounts is rendered by an alternative Greek vocabulary. In place of the usual Greek word for love, eros, the Greek translation of the Hebrew Bible and then the Greek New Testament used agape to designate at the same time the creating and redeeming love of God to the world and to humankind, the reciprocal love of humankind to God, and the love of persons as the witness of human love to God.

Agape is a comprehensive term including expressions of the above loves, which in the New Testament specifically expresses God's absolute and redemptive love shown in the person and work of Jesus Christ. Of the many Greek words for love, eros and agape have had particular significance for the Christian concept of love. It seems that agape was not a particularly significant part of the classical Greek religious and philosophical vocabulary of love. Lexicons such as Peters' *Greek Philosophical Terms* have extended entries on eros but not on agape. However, readers of the Greek New Testament have long been aware that agape is the dominant term for love in the Bible, and that eros does not appear in the texts at all. Assuming the writers of the Greek New Testament were self-conscious in their choice of vocabulary, the obvious question is why they chose the term agape and excluded the term eros. One reason may be that the term agape did not have the philosophical, religious, and ethical baggage associated with eros. In addition, the New Testament authors, themselves Jews, had ready to hand their Scripture, the Hebrew Bible, already in Greek translation. Known as the "Septuagint" or "LXX" in reference to the legendary number of 70 translators, this Greek translation of the "Old Testament," in circulation by around 100 BCE, used the term agape to translate the Hebrew words for love, "'aheb" and "hesed." While "'aheb" may refer to loving things, it is a comprehensive term for the reciprocal love between persons and that between God and people. Such reciprocal love is to be responsibly active in serving others and maintaining relationships. "Hesed" is that personal love that promotes the well-being of others. It is rooted in God's faithful and redeeming love, and thus is to act likewise toward others. Following the model of the Septuagint, the agape forms for love in the New Testament undergo a fundamental revaluation in relation to the common Greek language usage; the central meaning of love is set forth as the affection of persons to one another, God's affection to persons, and persons' affection to God.

There is no doubt that the biblical authors used the linguistic tools available to them, and that Greek was the common language of the Mediterranean world. The question, however, is whether the New Testament writers consciously used "agape" in contrast to "eros" in order to convey a specific theological meaning. Günther and Link in their article on love argue that they did: "It is because all human thought, feeling, action and worship are a response to a previous movement by God, that the LXX prefers the simpler word *agape* to the more loaded *eros*. The completely different direction of thought makes this quite understandable." This theologically informed choice was forcefully argued by Anders Nygren (1890–1978) in his study *Agape and Eros*. While Nygren was not the first to note the biblical use of agape for love, he so strongly emphasized the Christian use of agape and so sharply posed the historical–theological opposition of agape and eros, that nearly all consequent studies of the concept of love have reacted to his work.

In *Agape and Eros*, Nygren intended to set forth and to clarify the distinctive character of the Christian concept of love, agape, in contrast to the Greek concept of eros. Agape is primarily God's love, even when expressed by humans. Agape is a descending redemptive love, from God to humankind. Agape is completely unselfish; it is sacrificial giving. Agape loves the other and thereby creates value in the other. Eros, on the other hand, is acquisitive desire; it is the ascending movement of human attempts to reach God (however perceived). Eros is egocentric and is the highest form of self-assertion. It is primarily an acquisitive desire that loves its object for the value it sees in it. We might say that the opposition between agape and eros may be expressed with the theological epigram that salvation is received not achieved. We shall have the opportunity to discuss criticisms of Nygren's argument when we get to the modern period. For now, we may continue to reflect on the developing vocabulary of love.

By the early fourth century, the church had moved from a persecuted minority to an established position in the Roman Empire. Consequently the language of the Western church was no longer Greek but Latin. Latin did not possess the philosophical and literary distinctions of Greek. So, for example, the Greek eros and *philia* are both expressed by the Latin *amor*. Given the great importance of Scripture to Christianity, the first Latin Christian texts were most probably translations of the Bible. Agape was translated by three Latin words: *caritas*, *dilectio*, and *amor*. *Caritas* is the love of God and also ethical virtue. *Dilectio* is love in the sense of an act of the will on the basis of previous choice. The dominant word choice is *caritas*; *amor* is the least used for translating the Bible. *Dilectio* and *caritas* express the biblical law of love of God and neighbor. Latin-speaking Christians were accustomed to these words in reading and hearing Scripture. The words, while coming from profane Latin, now carried a new sense, a biblical sense of love.

In her massive study of the Latin vocabulary of Christian charity, Hélène Pétré argues that the early Christian claim of a new gospel required a new vocabulary to express that claim and its ramifications. Of course the early Christians were not privy to some special language but rather spoke the languages of their context, first Greek and then Latin. In the process of translating literally and theologically from Hebrew to Greek to

Latin, the authors of the Bible struggled to utilize the linguistic resources at their disposal. Later Christian writers, influenced by biblical vocabulary, continued this process of adapting profane language to evangelical usage. According to Pétré, the most characteristic example of the influence of the biblical text on the Christian sense of words is that of "caritas." *Caritas* was designated to translate the Greek *agape*. This old Latin word had a variety of senses: familial affection, friendship, sometimes patriotism. It took on the special sense of love of God and love of the neighbor for the Christians. At the same time it took on a rich religious and ethical content due to the frequency of its use in the Latin Bible. *Caritas* expressed in the least imperfectly possible way the nature of God of which the essential attribute is love: "God is caritas" (1 John 4:8,16). Hence the title of Pope Benedict XVI's 2006 encyclical, "Deus Caritas Est." *Caritas* expresses the incomprehensible benevolence of God for humankind: "See what caritatem the Father has given us" (1 John 3:1; cf. 3:16; 4:9, 16; Rom. 5:8; Eph. 2:4). *Caritas* sums up the entire Christian ethic, the law and the prophets, because the only thing demanded of the Christian is the two loves, the love of God and the love of others. *Caritas* is the compassionate and benevolent love for the poor; it is patience, mildness, unselfish (1 Cor. 13:4); it is dedicated to serve others (Gal. 5:13); it is mutual support (Eph. 4:2); it is the gift of the life that configures human love on the love of God (1 John 3:16).

These texts, as well as others, illustrate the change in import of the word from its profane to its religious sense. Vocabulary is formed in a word's usage, the resonance it evokes, its affective character, rather than solely in its unique intellectual content. There are splendid words, words that evoke an ideal and for that reason have a great expressive richness. This is so particularly in the language of a group. Words such as *caritas* gained a new quality in Christian language because they express a notion that is at the same time ethical and religious. The banal comparison of a society with a living organism, expressed by use of the word "corpus," picks up a completely special force and life when, following St. Paul, the church considers itself the "body of Christ," and Christians as "members of Christ." For the Christian community, *caritas* was not simply a human sentiment; it was the highest of the virtues for it conformed the person to God. Why did the word *caritas* itself and its synonyms so frequently recur in Christian authors if their religion was not, above all, the religion of love? It is not without interest for the history of ideas that this name was adopted by Christianity as that of the greatest and most characteristic of the virtues that it preached; it summed up all its ethics.

Toward the end of his *Confessions*, St. Augustine (354–430), the major theologian of Western Christianity, wrote: "Behold, the single love of God and of our neighbor, by what manifold sacraments and innumerable languages, and in each several language in how innumerable modes of speaking, it is bodily expressed." We shall next look at the "innumerable modes" of love expressed in the Bible.

Chapter 2

Biblical Views of Love

The concept of love in the Hebrew Bible reflects the development of biblical texts over a long period of time and in changing social and cultural contexts. Furthermore, the Hebrew Bible includes many types of literature: poetry, prophecy, wisdom, law codes, and narratives. Hence to assume that *a* concept of love can be abstracted or systematized from the rich and varied literature of the Hebrew Bible is misleading. A unified fundamental meaning of the Hebrew word-stem "to love" can hardly be determined because the concept covers a broad field of meaning ranging from preferences ("for he loved the soil," 2 Chron. 26:10) and proverbs ("Better is a dinner of vegetables where love is than a fatted ox and hatred with it," Prov. 15:17), to the erotic poetry of the Song of Songs ("Upon my bed at night I sought him whom my soul loves," 3:1), spousal affection ("Isaac...took Rebekah, and she became his wife; and he loved her," Gen. 24:67), and friendship ("Jonathan loved him [David] as his own soul," 1 Sam. 18:1), to God's love for his people ("When Israel was a child, I loved him," Hosea 11:1), for individual Israelites

("Jacob... the offspring of Abraham, my friend," Isa. 41:8), and occasionally for non-Israelites ("who loves the strangers," Deut. 10:18).

The setting for these many expressions of love is God's love for Israel manifest in their deliverance from bondage in Egypt. The constant refrain is "I am the Lord your God, who brought you out of Egypt, out of the house of slavery" (Exod. 20:2). God's choice of Israel is not dependent upon Israel's qualities but rather only upon God's love revealed in God's action (Deut. 7:7–11): "It was not because you were more numerous than any other people that the Lord set his heart on you and chose you.... It was because the Lord loved you and kept the oath that he swore to your ancestors, that the Lord has brought you out from the house of slavery." God's election of and covenant with the people places reciprocal obligations upon them: "Know therefore that the Lord your God is God, the faithful God who maintains covenant loyalty with those who love him and keep his commandments, to a thousand generations, and who repays in their own person those who reject him. Therefore, observe diligently the commandment – the statutes and the ordinances – that I am commanding you today."

Personal and social relationships are therefore rooted in the covenant and God's lordship: "You shall love your neighbor as yourself; I am the Lord" (Lev. 19:18). The love commandment forms a fundamental ethical norm for the social relationships of the Israelites. The neighbor is not just the fellow Israelite but also the non-Israelites who were already living in the land but were not integrated socially and religiously. The situation of these "aliens" is comparable to that of poor Israelites – neighbors to be loved, i.e., treated with respect and justice. "The alien who resides with you shall be to you as the citizen among you; you shall love the alien as yourself, for you were aliens in the land of Egypt. I am the Lord your God"

(Lev. 19:34). The Israelites are reminded that having experienced the condition of being aliens, it would be inconsistent to oppress aliens living among them. The self-communication formula – "I am the Lord" – that follows the injunctions of Leviticus 19 expresses both divine command and enablement.

Although some of the prophetic writings suggest that God's love is universal, extending to all peoples, the Hebrew Bible does not actually speak of the love of God reaching out beyond Israel. The command to love the alien appears to refer to the resident alien. Jenni states: "In contrast to the NT, the commandment remains limited to the 'compatriot'...and does not yet comprehend the whole ethic of communal behavior as a governing principle, as is already the case in the first part of the double commandment of love (Deut. 6:5) in relation to the behavior toward God."

The love relationship between God and Israel established by the deliverance from bondage in Egypt forms the repeated theme of the Hebrew Bible. It is frequently expressed in injunctions to righteous relationships; love and justice are interwoven. The Psalms, for example, continually present the intimate relationship of love and law, love and righteousness: "O Lord, I love the house in which you dwell, and the place where your glory abides" (Ps. 26:8); "He loves righteousness and justice; the earth is full of the steadfast love of the Lord" (Ps. 33:5); "As for me, I am poor and needy, but the Lord takes thought for me" (Ps. 40:17); "For God will save Zion . . . and those who love his name shall live in it" (Ps. 69:35–36); "He chose the tribe of Judah, Mount Zion, which he loves" (Ps. 78:68); "The Lord loves those who hate evil; he guards the lives of his faithful; he rescues them from the hand of the wicked" (Ps. 97:10); "Mighty King, lover of justice, you have established equity; you have executed justice and righteousness in Jacob" (Ps. 99:4); "I love the Lord, because he has heard my voice and supplications" (Ps. 116:1); and the long Psalm 119.

The God of Israel expects not just a portion but all of Israel's love: "Hear, O Israel: The Lord is our God, the Lord alone. You shall love the Lord your God with all your heart, and with all your soul, and with all your might" (Deut. 6:4–5). Love to God is not wordless rapture, but is reciprocal and capable of expression. Hence, God's commands and prohibitions shall be kept "in your heart," and publicly expressed and passed on to the next generation. "Recite them to your children and talk about them when you are at home and when you are away, when you lie down and when you rise. Bind them as a sign on your hand, fix them as an emblem on your forehead, and write them on the doorposts of your house and on your gates" (Deut. 6:7–9).

Moses makes it clear to the people that the relationship with God is not just a past event but a continuing, contemporary relationship. "The Lord our God made a covenant with us at Horeb. Not with our ancestors did the Lord make this covenant, but with us, who are all of us here alive today" (Deut. 5:2–3). As with any relationship, the partners are expected to remain faithful. "I the Lord your God am a jealous God, punishing children for the iniquity of parents, to the third and fourth generation of those who reject me, but showing steadfast love to the thousandth generation of those who love me and keep my commandments" (Deut. 5:9–10).

The biblical text goes on to narrate a rocky history of this love between God and his people. Time after time, the prophets warn of and then explicate the social and political catastrophes resulting from the people falling in love with false gods. These adulterous relationships, the breaking faith with the covenant, are evident in the oppression of the poor, the widow, and the orphan. The specifics of such self-aggrandizement in place of loving the neighbor as oneself are sharply and succinctly detailed in the book of Amos.

Marriage imagery for the relationship between God and Israel is developed in a startling way in the book of Hosea.

God tells Hosea to take a whore for a wife, and to have children by her as a parabolic action and metaphor for Israel's infidelity and God's faithfulness and love in spite of that infidelity. God's love for Israel is presented as a shocking defiance of convention. "Go, take for yourself a wife of whoredom and have children of whoredom, for the land commits great whoredom by forsaking the Lord" (Hosea 1:2). "The Lord said to me again, 'Go, love a woman who has a lover and is an adulteress, just as the Lord loves the people of Israel, though they turn to other gods...'" (Hosea 3:1). Israel's life arose out of God's love, a love that even as Israel falls into adultery cannot be turned aside. "When Israel was a child, I loved him, ... The more I called them, the more ... they kept sacrificing... to idols. How can I give you up,...?... I will not execute my fierce anger;... for I am God and no mortal, the Holy One in your midst, and I will not come in wrath" (Hosea 11:1–9). Els notes that marriage imagery signifies the personal quality of God's love, and that Hosea in chapter 11 "comes near to saying that God *is* love." Israel deserves destruction for faithlessness, yet God's love remains steadfast: "I will heal their disloyalty; I will love them freely, for my anger has turned from them" (Hosea 14:4).

While the people may not always remain faithful to God, God remains faithful to them. God's love is not eroded by the vagaries of human response but is the nature of God. "For the mountains may depart and the hills be removed, but my steadfast love shall not depart from you, and my covenant of peace shall not be removed, says the Lord, who has compassion on you" (Isa. 54:10); "I have loved you with an everlasting love; therefore I have continued my faithfulness to you" (Jer. 31:3). The prophets reiterate God's "gracious deeds... according to the abundance of his steadfast love" (Isa. 63:7). The future, according to Jeremiah, holds the promise of a new covenant. "It will not be like the covenant that I made with their ancestors when I took them by the hand to bring them out of the land of Egypt – a covenant that they broke, though I was their husband, says the Lord. . . . I will put my law within them, and I will write it on their hearts; and I will be their God, and they shall be my people. No longer shall they teach one another, or say to each other, 'Know the Lord,' for they shall all know me, from the least of them to the greatest, says the Lord; for I will forgive their iniquity, and remember their sins no more" (Jer. 31:31–34). The sovereign God who in his love relationship to Israel tolerates no third party, is at the same time ready to be entirely Israel's life.

What then is Israel's life in love with God to be? It is clearly not a life of sentimentality or ecstasy but rather an ethical life. The idea of a subjective feeling of love for God is rare. The Bible as a whole does not advance the mystical religiosity that permeates classical Greek religion. Likewise, the Bible does not promote mystical union with God through the rituals of nature religions. The Hebrew Bible records ongoing attacks on the Canaanite fertility cults revolving around Baal worship with its phallic symbols of pillars and its sacred prostitution. "You must demolish completely all the places where the nations whom you are about to dispossess served their gods, . . . Break down their altars, smash their pillars, burn their sacred poles . . ." (Deut. 12:2–3; cf. also 2 Kings 23: 4–15). Unlike the ancient Near Eastern divinization of natural forces with the assumption that sex is a primary principle of generation in both creation and divinity, the Hebrew Bible does not attribute sexual characteristics and functions to God. In the Bible, humankind does not ascend to God by any means; rather, God chooses humankind. The article on love by Günther and Link echoes the contrast of eros and agape mentioned earlier. "In the OT [Old Testament] man can never ascend to God; in the Gk. [Greek] understanding of *eros* he can."

God's love to Israel judges as well as forgives Israel's aberrations from the divine standards of justice set forth in the commandments (Exod. 20:1–17; Deut. 5:6–21) and summarized in the phrase "you shall love your neighbor as yourself" (Lev. 19:18). Verse 34 adds the "alien" to neighbor: "you shall love the alien as yourself." The broad semantic range for "neighbor," generally meaning a person of the covenant community, gave rise to extended discussions of its meaning as may be seen in the lawyer's question to Jesus, "Who is my neighbor?" (Luke 10:29). The "alien" (also "sojourner," "resident alien," "stranger") usually meant a non-Israelite living in Israel. The love that requires accountability includes that between parents and children. "Those who spare the rod hate their children, but those who love them are diligent to discipline them" (Prov. 13:24).

Love to the neighbor is not only the grateful response to God's love for Israel, it is also commanded in two specific texts: Deut. 10:19 and Lev. 19:18, 34. Thus love to God and the neighbor is far more than an emotion; it is behavior. Love to the neighbor as oneself is a communal ethos that in principle summarizes and extends individual commandments. This love, understood as mutual solidarity within the community, is directed to the adult citizens and requires them to protect the dignity and substance of the ethnic group.

The prophets never tire of proclaiming responsibility to care for the least in the community. "Wash yourselves; make yourselves clean; remove the evil of your doings from before my eyes; cease to do evil, learn to do good; seek justice, rescue the oppressed, defend the orphan, plead for the widow" (Isa. 1:16–17). True worship is not "solemn assemblies" and "offerings," but justice. "I take no delight in your solemn assemblies. Even though you offer me your burnt offerings and grain offerings, I will not accept them; . . . But let justice roll down like waters, and righteousness like an everflowing stream" (Amos 5:21–24).

Jenni makes the point that the reference to self-love in Lev. 19:18, 34 "is simply presupposed as the norm" not "as a dangerous temptation one must combat through self-denial." Love is self-explanatory; persons are referred to what they already know. In contrast, then, to the Western cultural interest in introspection and conscience, the biblical reference to self-love appears in the pre-Freudian context of covenant rather than emotion and self-regard. In his extensive study of Lev. 19:18, Mathys persuasively argues that this is the correct insight into the famous friendship of David and Jonathan (1 Sam. 18:1, 3; 19:1; 20:17; 2 Sam. 1:26). Jonathan, the son of King Saul, is the one who initiates the pact to protect the future king, David.

We mentioned above that biblical religion continually sought to separate (the root sense of the words "elect" and "holy") itself from the fertility and mystery religions of its context. In relation to love between persons the Hebrew Bible strips sexual relations of the numinous religious character that Israel's sexual-mythical environment attributed to them. In contrast to the Baal religious orientation, the Bible celebrates the joy of sex without supernatural baggage. Sexual relations are not means to self-transcendence and ascent to the divine or by sympathetic magic means to influence the fertility of crops and animals upon which agricultural peoples are so dependent. Sex is not a divine principle but simply part of the creation. Again, in contrast to the mythologies of the ancient world, the creation stories in Genesis 1–2 declare God made humans in two sexes to be companions. Woman is created as the fit partner with man, with human dignity, equally blessed by God (Gen. 1:27–28). The strength of sexual attraction is clearly set forth in such stories as Isaac and Rebekah (Gen. 24:62–67) among others, not to mention Jacob who spent 14 years serving his future father-in-law in order to win the hand of Rachel (Gen. 29:18–30)! The biblical celebration of sexual love is famously expressed in the Song of Songs, also known as the Song of Solomon. The Song of Songs echoes ancient Egyptian love poetry in celebrating the sensual pleasures of human sexual relationships. Medieval efforts either to moralize and allegorize away the erotic dimension of the Song of Songs or to link sex to salvation distort the poetry.

At the same time, while human love is not spiritualized it is ethical. The intoxication of sexual love, "better than wine" (Song of Sol. 1:2, 4; 4:10; 5:1; 7:13), is not an excuse or reason for adulterous behavior. "Rejoice in the wife of your youth, ... may her breasts satisfy you at all times; may you be intoxicated always by her love. Why should you be intoxicated, my son, by another woman and embrace the bosom of an adulteress? For human ways are under the eyes of the Lord, and he examines all their paths" (Prov. 5:18–21). That no one is above the law, including the king, is clear by the judgment of David for taking the wife of another, Bathsheba (2 Sam. 11–13). The God whose covenant manifests his steadfast love to the people, expects the people to be faithful to that covenant love and in turn to manifest it in relation to others. Consonant with this orientation, the institution of marriage is not constituted primarily by love as an emotion but by faithfulness to the covenant of marriage.

In the New Testament, as in the Hebrew Bible, love is grounded in God's self-revelation. Leaving aside historical questions of Jesus' self-understanding, his words, and the event of Easter, the New Testament texts present Jesus as the definitive revelation of God's love (John 3:16; Rom. 5:8; 1 John 4:8–10). On the eve of the crucifixion, the Fourth Gospel presents Jesus saying to his disciples:

> As the Father has loved me, so I have loved you; abide in my love. If you keep my commandments, you will abide in my love, just as I have kept my Father's commandments and abide

in his love.... This is my commandment, that you love one another as I have loved you. No one has greater love than this, to lay down one's life for one's friends. You are my friends if you do what I command you.... You did not choose me but I chose you. And I appointed you to go and bear fruit, fruit that will last, so that the Father will give you whatever you ask him in my name. I am giving you these commands so that you may love one another.

(John 15:9–17)

The love that is expected of the disciples has its basis and its model in Jesus' love to them. The commandment to love is part of a comprehensive theological conception of love that is modeled on God's covenantal love and the response to it presented in Israel's fundamental confession: "Hear, O Israel: The Lord is our God, the Lord alone. You shall love the Lord your God with all your heart, and with all your soul, and with all your might" (Deut. 6:4–5).

Again, the biblical *commandment* to love the neighbor is not contingent upon spontaneous personal affections, religious transformation, or the lovability of the neighbor, especially if perceived as an enemy. The commandment to love is a commandment precisely because it is rooted in God and is God's continual word of judgment and reconciliation to the human failure to love. In the words of Victor Furnish: "When love is presented in the New Testament as the sovereign command of a sovereign Lord, then it becomes evident that it is the divine love alone which is regarded as the measure and meaning of love's claim." Furnish continues, "Therefore, to hear that love command is to be called to repentance.... Yet because the infinite demand of love formulated into this commandment has its origin and context in the infinite love of God, the one under command knows that he stands not only under judgment, but under grace. The command discloses not only the depth of man's sin and the seriousness of his alienation from true life, but also the depth of God's forgiving love and the seriousness of the divine purpose to save."

Jesus' continuity and discontinuity with his religious tradition appears throughout the New Testament. For example, his emphasis upon love for God reiterates his Scripture, the Hebrew Bible. Jesus replies to the question of which commandment is the greatest by combining Deut. 6:4–5, cited above, with Lev. 19:18, "You shall love your neighbor as yourself." "On these two commandments hang all the law and the prophets" (Matt. 22:40; cf. Mark 12:28–34; Luke 10:25–28). At the same time Jesus directs love of the neighbor beyond cultic restriction and beyond the circle of compatriots. To the old question of who is my neighbor, Jesus tells the story of the Good Samaritan (Luke 10:29–37). Whoever is in need is the neighbor. The tradition is further shattered when the religious people, the priest and Levite, do not help but the alien Samaritan does what has to be done for the wounded man.

The implication of the parable that God's love includes everyone, including notorious sinners and enemies, is spelled out elsewhere. The account of the woman sinner who anoints Jesus' feet with oil (Luke 7:36–50) connects love and forgiveness: " 'her sins, which were many, have been forgiven; hence she has shown great love. But the one to whom little is forgiven, loves little.' Then he said to her, 'Your sins are forgiven.' But those who were at table with him began to say among themselves, 'Who is this who even forgives sins?' "

In the demand to love one's enemies, Jesus radicalized the law. In a series following the Beatitudes (Matt. 5:3–12), Jesus sets forth the demands of a new age with the formula "You have heard that it was said to those of ancient times. . . . But I say to you." The old age forbade murder, the new forbids anger and disparagement; the old age forbade adultery, the new forbids lust; the old age posited controlled retaliation, the new promotes non-retaliation. The series ends: "You have heard that it was said, 'You shall love your neighbor and hate your enemy.' But I say to you, Love your enemies and pray for those who persecute you, ... For if you love those who love you, what reward have you? Do not even the tax collectors do the same? And if you salute only your brethren, what more are you doing than others? Do not even the Gentiles do the same?" (Matt. 5:43–47). The parallel in Luke reads: "If you love those who love you, what credit is that to you? For even sinners love those who love them. And if you do good to those who do good to you, what credit is that to you? For even sinners do the same. ... But love your enemies, and do good, and lend, expecting nothing in return; and your reward will be great, ... Be merciful, even as your Father is merciful" (Luke 6:32–36; see also Rom. 12:14–20; 1 Thess. 5:15; 1 Pet. 3:9).

According to Piper, there are not sufficient sources in either Stoic–Hellenistic literature nor in the Hebrew Bible and Jewish literature to establish any of these literatures as the origin for the command to love one's enemies. His analysis of the Sermon on the Mount argues that the essential historical origin of the command to love one's enemies can only be possible as part of the proclamation of Jesus. "That which sets the early church off from its environment ... is that which it has in common with Jesus."

The new demand to love even one's enemies is set in the context of Jesus' proclamation of God's love and mercy that in forgiving sins creates a new situation that enables love to others including outcasts such as lepers (Luke 5:12–15; see Lev. 13–14) and "tax collectors and sinners" (the former collaborated with the Roman authorities and thus were viewed as treasonous and exploitative; the latter is a collective term for those whose work made them ritually unclean). Jesus' answer to the question put by the Pharisees and scribes, "Why do you eat and drink with tax collectors and sinners?" is "Those who are well have no need of a physician, but those who are sick; I have not come to call the righteous, but sinners to repentance" (Luke 5:29–32). This agape love is distinguished from the love of friends that is reciprocal, mutual liking, by its gratuitousness or disinterestedness. That is, agape love is not dependent upon results.

God's love presented as forgiveness and mercy is not just his disposition, a kind of divine "stock in trade," but it is an ethical love that demands and well as enables. God's unconditional love for sinners calls sinners to respond with unconditional love for others. God's love, Jesus proclaims, creates a new situation, new responsibilities as well as possibilities. The New Testament writers apply this love to Jesus himself; i.e., Jesus the one who proclaims the love of God becomes the one who is proclaimed to be the love of God. Hence love of the least is love of Jesus and neglect of the least is neglect of Jesus. At the Last Judgment, the nations will be separated "as a shepherd separates the sheep from the goats." "Then the King will say to those at his right hand, 'Come, O blessed of my Father, inherit the kingdom prepared for you from the foundation of the world; for I was hungry and you gave me food, I was thirsty and you gave me drink, I was a stranger and you welcomed me, I was naked and you clothed me, I was sick and you visited me, I was in prison and you came to me.' " The righteous are clueless and the King then says, "Truly, I say to you, as you did it to one of the least of these my brethren, you did it to me." The King then addresses those at his left hand: "Depart from me, you cursed, into the eternal fire prepared for the devil and his angels; for I was hungry and you gave me no food, I was thirsty and you gave me no drink, I was a stranger and you did not welcome me, naked and you did not clothe me, sick and in prison and you did not visit me." The unrighteous are equally clueless, and are told: "Truly, I say to you, as you did it not to one of the least of these, you did it not to me" (Matt. 25:31–46). The essence of faith in Jesus as the Christ is that it is active in love (Gal. 5:6).

In his letter to the Romans, Paul emphasizes "God's love poured into our hearts." "God proves his love for us in that while we still were sinners Christ died for us" (Rom. 5:5–8). Indeed, Paul proclaims, "we are more than conquerors through him who loved us. For I am convinced that neither death, nor life, nor angels, nor rulers, nor things present, nor things to come, nor powers, nor height, nor depth, nor anything else in all creation, will be able to separate us from the love of God in Christ Jesus our Lord" (Rom. 8:37–39).

Consistent with the other New Testament writings, Paul's understanding of ethics flows from his conviction of the priority of God's love. "[O]ne who loves another has fulfilled the law. The commandments...are summed up in this word, 'Love your neighbor as yourself.' Love does no wrong to a neighbor; therefore, love is the fulfilling of the law" (Rom. 13:8–10). "[T]hrough love become slaves to one another. For the whole law is summed up in a single commandment, 'You shall love your neighbor as yourself' " (Gal. 5:13–14). "So let us not grow weary in doing what is right, for we will reap at harvest-time, if we do not give up. So then, whenever we have an opportunity, let us work for the good of all, and especially for those of the family of faith" (Gal. 6:9–10). It is of interest that Paul rarely speaks of love for God. Rather, the agape that flows from God is directed to service to the neighbor.

The question now is, what is that service to the neighbor? What is the content of that love, agape? It clearly is not "wickedness, evil, covetousness, malice,...envy, murder, strife, deceit, craftiness," nor is it gossip, slander, hatred of God, insolence, pride, ruthlessness and heartlessness (Rom. 1:29–31). "Love is patient; love is kind; love is not envious or boastful or arrogant or rude. It does not insist on its own way; it is not irritable or resentful; it does not rejoice in wrongdoing, but rejoices in the truth. It bears all things, believes all things, hopes all things, endures all things. Love never ends" (1 Cor. 13:4–8; cf. Gal. 5:18–26; Rom. 12:9–21). Love is at the same time God's action toward humankind and the human answer to it.

God's love liberates the person from that calculating frame of mind that accompanies human efforts to attain success however defined. The freedom of the Christian, Paul reminds his Galatians, is not the occasion for self-aggrandizement but the fulfillment of Lev. 19:18. "For you were called to freedom, brothers and sisters; only do not use your freedom as an opportunity for self-indulgence, but through love become slaves to one another. For the whole law is summed up in a single commandment, 'You shall love your neighbor as yourself' " (Gal. 5:13–14; Rom. 13:8–10). Furthermore, Paul does not limit this to the Christian community; it is a universal responsibility derived from God's saving activity: "So then, whenever we have an opportunity, let us work for the good of all, and especially for those of the family of faith" (Gal. 6:10; cf. Rom. 12:9–21). Within these parameters, the believer is to love in the concrete circumstances of his or her life, "testing everything" to figure out what the good is in the particular situation that will build up the person and the community (1 Thess. 5:21).

One New Testament letter, according to Theissen, that provides a powerful model of early Christian ethics based on love is the letter of James. For the author of James, the commandment to love is inextricable from treating each person, including those outside the Christian community, on an equal footing. The biblical injunction to love the neighbor as oneself is understood in James to entail the renunciation of one's rank so that love is more than merciful condescension to the needy or deference to the superior.

> My brethren, show no partiality as you hold the faith of
> our Lord Jesus Christ, the Lord of glory. For if a man with
> gold rings and in fine clothing comes into your assembly, and
> a poor man in shabby clothing also comes in, and you pay
> attention to the one who wears the fine clothing and say,
> "Have a seat here, please," while you say to the poor man,
> "Stand there," or "Sit at my feet," have you not made distinc-
> tions among yourselves, and become judges with evil thoughts?
>   (James 2:1–4)

The commandment of love implies the commandment of
impartiality, of equality, "for God shows no partiality"
(James 2:11).

When James refers to the socially and economically marginalized as "brothers and sisters" he is conferring upon them
a fundamentally egalitarian status that he intends literally
and not in word only. "If a brother or sister is ill-clad and
in lack of daily food, and one of you says to them, 'Go in
peace, be warmed and filled,' without giving them the things
needed for the body, what does it profit? So faith by itself, if it
has no works is dead" (James 2:15–17; cf. Rom. 2:13). It is
important to note that James is not speaking of requests by the
needy but rather the very existence of poverty that must incite
response. Furthermore, the community as a whole is to alleviate need wherever seen; this is a collective work to which
each contributes. "Religion that is pure and undefiled before
God and the Father is this: to visit orphans and widows in their
affliction, and to keep oneself unstained from the world"
(James 1:27), that is, the "world" as socio-economic hierarchy
opposing God's equitable love (cf. James 4:13–5:6). That such
love was understood to be counter-cultural may be seen in the
Gospels' "great reversal" theme where the first shall be last
and the last first as well as in "the Magnificat" (Luke 1:46–55)
where Mary speaks of the humbling of the powerful and the

lifting of the lowly; the feeding of the hungry and the exile of the rich.

Similar conviction is expressed in 1 John 3:11–23:

> For this is the message you have heard from the beginning, that we should love one another. . . . We know that we have passed from death to life because we love one another. Whoever does not love abides in death. . . . We know love by this, that he laid down his life for us [cf. John 3:16] – and we ought to lay down our lives for one another. How does God's love abide in anyone who has the world's goods and sees a brother or sister in need and yet refuses to help? Little children, let us love, not in word or speech, but in truth and action.

A more comprehensive review of the New Testament writings concerned with "love" would further emphasize what we have already seen in these selected texts: love (agape) is first of all God's gift and then the responsibility of Christians. Without the transcendent theological understanding of love, the ethical meaning of love would lose its enabling foundation. Love as community with God is the driving force and creative origin of the concrete, demanded love to others. The English language may promote a tendency to linear thinking about this relationship of God's love to love of the neighbor. Hence, our reflection may be enriched by recalling how another language, in this case German, provides word plays that hold these loves together and suggest their dialectical relationship. In German, "Gabe" means gift and "Auf*gabe*" means duty or responsibility; note that "gift" is embedded in "duty." Likewise, in the set of words "Wort" (word), "Ant*wort*" (answer), and "Verant*wort*ung" (responsibility) we may play with the relationship of God's Word, human response and responsibility seeing the centrality of God's Word in human answer and life.

Chapter 3

A World Without Love?
The Greco-Roman World and
Early Christianity

Gerhard Uhlhorn, in his magisterial three-volume study of the history of Christian charity, described the Greco-Roman context for Christianity as "a world without love." Uhlhorn (1826–1901) was motivated to undertake his study by a conversation with Theodor Fliedner (1800–1864), the "father" of the modern deaconess movement and a leader in the development of social welfare. Fliedner had urged Uhlhorn to write the history of Christian charity in order to awaken and increase contemporary works of love in the context of the social ills of the Industrial Revolution. Given Uhlhorn's intent to present the history of Christian love, his judgment of the Greco-Roman world may appear both harsh and suspect. His point, however, was not that pre-Christian Greeks and Romans had no inkling of love but that their understanding of love did not envision love beyond one's own circle or status for the well being of others.

The Roman dramatist, Plautus (c.254–184 BCE) wrote: "A man is a wolf to a man whom he does not know." Aid to the poor was seen as useless because it could not elevate them to the level of the rich and thereby grant happiness. Indeed, it was said that assistance to the poor is not only a waste of effort but is no favor to the poor because it only extends their miserable lives. Plautus, again: "What is given to the poor is lost." And: "He deserves ill of a beggar who gives him food and drink. For that which is given is thrown away, and the life of the beggar is protracted to his misery." Plato's ideal state according the *Republic* has no room for the poor; beggars are to be expelled. If a worker is ill, there is no obligation to assist him; if he can no longer work, he is a drain on the state and his life has no value.

Greek and Roman attitudes shared a general disdain for the "least" in society, for women, the weak, and the marginalized. The Roman city-state did, however, strive to inculcate a sense of civic responsibility and social stability through contributions from the wealthy. The supremacy of the emperor and the well-being of the upper class depended at least to some extent upon the loyalty of the populace, and that loyalty in part at least rested upon received or anticipated benefits. Nobles, office-holders, and priests were to provide support for buildings, feasts, grain doles, and entertainments. The expectation of beneficence was supported by the promise of honor. If one did not give when expected, the consequence was *infamia*, that is, disgrace, dishonor. *Fama*, on the other hand, was the favorable public reputation, even glory, that the noble person strove for and that was attainable through that gift-giving so important to ancient culture. As Countryman points out, "It is not surprising, under the circumstances, that the fundamental motive for philanthropy was *philotimia*, 'love of public recognition.'"

While honor is an evident motivation for the "philanthropy" of the wealthy, there is little evidence of pity or compassion for the poor in ancient culture. In the ancient world, one gave in order to get. As mentioned earlier, eudaemonism is a perspective that defines the ethical life in relation to happiness or personal well-being. In Plato's *Symposium*, eudaemonism is the love-impelled ascent toward the good and immortality. But even with Plato's refined eudaemonism, the chief benefit of such love is always one's own benefit. As developed by Aristotle, the point of friendship and generous benevolence is the decorous conduct worthy of a noble person. Classical Greco-Roman understanding of "charity" focused only upon those of equal status with a view to advantage. The Aristotelian view was that wealth is useful in securing friendships not in just being amassed. The point of view was the reciprocity of the *do ut des* principle, "I give that you may give." This principle of quid pro quo that posited an equivalent return could be conceived as a contract in which each party gives and receives an equivalent. Hence, the Greek historian Polybius (c.205–c.123 BCE) stated that "nobody ever gives anything of his own willingly to anybody." The *do ut des* principle, according to Kudlein, formed with individual nuances the basis of pre-Christian teaching and praxis of friendship. Thus the physician, according to the Roman Stoic philosopher Seneca (c.4 BCE–65 CE), could be conceived as the "friend" of the patient, but could never be conceived of as the "friend" or "benefactor" of the poor. The explicit "physician of the poor" has its roots in the *philoptochía*, the *amor pauperum*, "love of the poor," of early Christianity. Thus early Christendom was particularly attractive to the poor. Nock emphasized that "a poor man must have gained a great sense of security" through belonging to a Christian community.

Benevolence gained honor, friendship, and business. Hence the Roman statesman, Cicero (106–43 BCE) remarked that most people are generous for the sake of honor: "What is given to friends is outside fortune's grasp." The inscriptions of the ancient world testify to Cicero's point. Hands' volume, *Charities and Social Aid in Greece and Rome*, provides examples. A second-century-BCE inscription celebrates Apollonius, son of Hierokles of Miletus, a doctor who served "the people freely during the six month period of office; and in as much as he did this with his heart set upon honor...he is awarded an encomium to encourage further service, also an olive wreath... [and an inscription] on a stone which is to be placed in the temple of Poseidan and Amphritite." An inscription of about the same time speaks of another doctor, Menokritos, who continued "his energetic service in his love of honor." Around 100 BCE, Theopompos, "maintaining the good relations with the people inherited from his ancestors, and seeking further to increase his right-dealing with gods and men, having zealously pursued the life of virtue and honour from his earliest youth...[leaves] an imperishable memorial for all time of his noble spirit and goodwill for the people...the purchase of [anointing] oil for the gymnasium...." Theopompos as a result was awarded "a gold crown and two bronze statues with honorary inscription; the decree itself to be inscribed on two stone monuments; public proclamation of these honours at festivals of Dionysos and of Artemis; inscriptions also to be added to the statues of sons and daughters set up by Theopompos." Even more explicit is the intention expressed by a wealthy man of the second century CE: "I wish my gift and favour...to be published on three marble pillars; of these, one should be set up...in the market before my house, and one should be erected in the *Caesereum*, set close by the gates of the temple, and one in the gymnasium, so that to both the citizens of Gytheion, and to the non-citizens, my philanthropic and kindly act may be clear and well-known to all.... My idea is to achieve immortality in making such a just and kindly disposal [of my property] and, in entrusting it to the city, I shall surely not fail in my aim." The Roman orator, Pliny the Younger (c.62–c.114 CE) asked what could be greater than glory and praise for all eternity. To which question Tertullian (c.160–c.225 CE), the African church father and first major theologian to write in Latin, retorted: "You pour forth statues and inscribe sculptured images and have your honorary epitaphs, reading 'to the eternal memory of...' Why, as far as it lies in your power, you yourselves provide a kind of resurrection for the dead."

The historian de Ste. Croix has argued that "the graeco-roman world was obsessively concerned with wealth and status.... But wealth was by far the most important determinant of status. Ovid put it beautifully... 'it is property that confers rank'...." Ste. Croix goes on to point out that classical socio-economic vocabulary was weighted with moral values that portrayed the wealthy and powerful as good and the lower classes as bad. "The Roman governing class was as thoroughly devoted to property as the most wealth-conscious of the Greeks. No surviving Greek writer was as thoroughly devoted to the over-riding importance of property rights as Cicero...." Biblical language turned these values upside down by often associating the poor and marginalized with moral virtues and the wealthy and powerful with corruption. The early church also reversed the Greco-Roman view of wealth. According to Tertullian, among others, ambition and desire for glory were vices; the drive for social recognition was in strict opposition to Christian humility, and the goal of social recognition is a typical mark of the social-climber mentality.

The poor obviously did not have such means to the honor and fame their society prized, and thus were often scorned. Cicero called the poor "the scum of the city" who, he said, should be skimmed off and sent to the colonies. Since, to the Romans "property confers rank," their devotion to property rights granted an owner the right not only to the use of his property – including slaves – but also to its abuse or even destruction. Since wealth was an important determinant of status, Greek vocabulary began giving moral weight to socio-economic terminology. Words for property-owning – rich, fortunate, distinguished, well-born, influential – also had moral connotations of the good, the best, upright, fair-minded. Words for the lower classes of people – the poor, the mob, the populace – had negative moral connotations. In classical antiquity there was no pity for the destitute. The reigning ideology was that the gods love the wealthy.

Education and health care depended upon philanthropy. Civic support of education and health care was limited to soldiers and their families. There may perhaps have been free medical treatment at the temples of Aescaplius, the god of physicians, but there were no hospitals in the ancient world. "Public service doctors" in ancient Greece meant only certification by the polis not that there was free medical attention. Those with long-term illness, the deformed, the handicapped, and "surplus" children were not considered worthy of care by society. Plato, for example, had little patience for the chronically ill; medical resources should be for those who can return to a productive life.

In his pioneering study on the early spread of Christianity, Adolf von Harnack attributes the expansion of Christianity in the early centuries to its faith being active in love; the Christians not only had a new vocabulary of love, they lived it. "The new language on the lips of Christians was the language of love. But it was more than a language, it was a thing of power and action.... The gospel thus became a social message." Even the Greek satirist and scoffer of all time, Lucian of Samosata (c.120–c.200), while ridiculing Christian beliefs in Jesus, conceded their love of one another to the extent of sparing no expense.

In the early church, worship, liturgy, and love for the neighbor were seen as inseparable. The exercise of love to the neighbor was intrinsic to every Christian community that desired to remain true to the gospel. Again Harnack: "Brotherliness is love on a footing of equality; ministering love means to give and to forgive, and no limit to this is to be recognized. Besides, ministering love is the practical expression of love to God." Of the numerous writings testifying to this connection Justin Martyr (c.100–c.165) and Tertullian provide representative examples. Justin, who literally lost his head for love, was one of the first Christian thinkers to defend the faith to the emperor and the Roman Senate. He described the weekly liturgy of scripture readings, sermons, sacrament, and offering. The offering is voluntary: "And they who are well to do, and willing, give what each thinks fit; and what is collected is deposited with the president [i.e., bishop], who succors the orphans and widows, and those who, through sickness or any other cause, are in want, and those who are in bonds, and the strangers sojourning among us, and in a word takes care of all who are in need."

Tertullian linked worship and love of neighbor in contrast to his culture: "Though we have our treasure chest, it is not made up of purchase-money, as of a religion that has its price [i.e., we don't have to pay to worship]. On the monthly day, if he likes, each puts in a small donation; but only if it be his pleasure, and only if he be able: for there is no compulsion; all is voluntary. These gifts are, as it were, piety's deposit fund. For they are not taken thence and spent on feasts, and drinking bouts, and eating-houses, but to support and bury poor people, to supply the wants of boys and girls destitute of means and parents, and of old persons confined now to the house; such, too, as have suffered shipwreck; and if there happen to be any in the mines, or banished to the islands, or shut up in the prisons, for nothing but their fidelity to the cause of God's

Church, they become the nurslings of their confession. But it is mainly the deeds of love so noble that lead many to put a brand upon us. 'See,' they say, 'how they love one another,'...." In response to the charge that Christianity was eroding the old cults, Tertullian responded: "[Y]ou say, the temple revenues are falling off [due to the growth of the church]: how few now throw in a contribution! In truth, we are not able to give alms both to your human and your heavenly mendicants; nor do we think that we are required to give to any but to those who ask for it. Let Jupiter then hold out his hand and get, for our compassion spends more in the streets than yours does in the temples."

Clement of Alexandria (c.150–c.215), who became head of the famous Catechetical School there, wrote in his *Paedagogus,* a tract on Christian life: "Even as such wells as spring up, rise to their formal level even after they have been drained, so that kindly spring of love to men, the bestowal of gifts, imparts its drink to the thirsty, and is again increased and replenished." Love to the neighbor is not dependent upon the neighbor's character but that person's needs. Chrysostom (c.347–407), bishop of Constantinople, stated that "alms are to be given, not to the way of life, but to the human being; we must have compassion, not because the poor are virtuous, but because they are needy." The clarity of Chrysostom's preaching led to his exile and death.

All Christians were called upon to assist "the least" in society. In this respect fasting or choosing less expensive food such as fish was recommended as a means to save expenses in order to provide assistance to those in greater need. As the examples illustrate, the early church did not think its works of love were limited to personal almsgiving. A church fund, literally a "common chest," *arca* in Tertullian's Latin, associated charity very closely with worship and the church leaders, bishops and deacons. The bishop is among other things to be a "lover of the poor." The deacons are to ascertain who are in distress and not exclude them from a share in the church funds. The gifts of money and in kind (bread, wine, oil, cheese, olives, fruits, vegetables – even flowers) were brought to the worship service and entrusted to the bishop, by whom they were placed on the altar and thus consecrated to God. All these goods were understood as nothing else than the gifts of God which should be distributed to the needy. Hence, the recipients received these gifts from the hand of God. Recipients were designated by the bishop with the advice of the deacons who were expected to be familiar with local needs. The deacons were responsible for distributing the money and goods both at the close of worship and to the homes of the needy. The office of the deacon since the second century was twofold: assisting the bishop in the liturgy of the Lord's Supper, and extending that worship in a "liturgy after the liturgy" in service to the needy. Through the mediation of the deacons daily life was moved to the center of worship and worship was extended into daily life.

A memorable story of one of those deacons is that of St. Laurence, a Roman deacon. A tradition stemming from St. Ambrose (c.339–397) presented Laurence (d. 258) as the exemplar for selling the church's liturgical art and treasure in order to provide for the poor. When confronted by the Roman prefect who demanded Laurence turn over the church's treasure, he assembled the poor of his parish to whom he had distributed the church's wealth, and explained that the poor were the true treasure of the church. The Roman official was not amused, and legend has it that Laurence was slowly roasted to death on a gridiron. That Laurence was probably beheaded instead does not diminish the point that Laurence illustrated the Christian conviction that God's love is active toward the least of society. The action of Laurence was a model of love for others: Ambrose, bishop of Milan (c.339–397), and also Deogratias, archbishop of Carthage (454–477), used church wealth to redeem captives after the collapse of the Pax Romana, as did also St. Augustine, bishop of Hippo (354–430). St. Cyril (c.315–386), bishop of Jerusalem, sold liturgical art to provide food for the poor. Riquet cites Ambrose: "The goods of the Church are the patrimony of the poor. Tell me, if you can, what prisoners the pagan temples have ransomed, what poor folk they have fed, what exiles they have supported?" Rudolph provides an historical overview of these actions into the Middle Ages including the story of a monk who sold his only possession, a copy of the Gospels, in order to feed the poor, "thus selling the Word which commanded him to sell all and give to the poor."

It was common in the early centuries to follow the worship service with what we might today call a potluck meal. Significantly, for our discussion, it was called a love feast, an agape meal. Some of the aspersions that Romans cast on Christianity focused on the agape meal with claims that it was an occasion for immorality. Tertullian asks why there should be any surprise that people in love should eat in common. After all, he wrote, the Greek Socrates and the Roman Cato shared their wives with their friends!

> O noble example of Attic wisdom, of Roman gravity – the philosopher and the censor playing pimps! What wonder if that great love of Christians towards one another is desecrated by you! For you abuse also our humble feasts, on the ground that they are extravagant as well as infamously wicked. . . . Our feast explains itself by its name. The Greeks call it agape, i.e., affection. Whatever it costs, our outlay in the name of piety is gain, since with the good things of the feast we benefit the needy; not as it is with you . . . but as it is with God himself, a peculiar respect is shown to the lowly. . . . As an act of religious service, it permits no vileness or immodesty. The participants, before reclining, taste first of prayer to God. As much is eaten as satisfies the cravings of hunger; as much is drunk as befits the

chaste. They say it is enough, as those who remember that even during the night they have to worship God; they talk as those who know that the Lord is one of their auditors.

As if to contrast the agape feast with Plato's *Symposium*, Tertullian concludes: "We go from it, not like troops of mischief-doers, nor bands of vagabonds, nor to break out into licentious acts, but to have as much care of our modesty and chastity as if we had been at a school of virtue rather than a banquet."

Harrison notes that the "Church's care for the needy, for foundlings, widows, the poor, although it had Jewish roots, was new and striking affirmation of a common humanity shared by all, rich and poor, in the traditionally hierarchic context of late antique society." The Christians' love for the poor exhibited through the charity of the church made a deep impression in the Roman Empire and contributed to the growth of the church. This is clearly seen in the action of the Emperor Julian (332–363), known as Julian the Apostate because upon becoming emperor in 360 he renounced the Christian faith in which he was reared and embarked upon a campaign to reinstate worship of the old gods of the empire. Rejecting open persecution of the church, Julian strove to displace it by co-opting its social concern. One of Julian's letters, provided by Kidd, noted that Christianity was spreading because of its love for the neighbor. "I think the impious Galileans [i.e., Christians] have observed this fact [pagan neglect of the poor] and devoted themselves to philanthropy. And they have gained ascendancy in the worst of their deeds through the credit they win for such practices. . . . [T]he Galileans also begin with their so-called love-feast ["the agape"], or hospitality, or service of tables – for they have many ways of carrying it out, and hence call it by many names – and the result is that they have led very many into atheism [i.e., rejection of the gods of Hellenism]." Julian, as Pontifex Maximus, High Priest of the Empire, wrote to the High Priest of the province of Galatia: "If our religion does not make the progress we could wish, the blame lies with those who profess it. The gods have done great things for us, . . . But is it right that we should be satisfied with their favors, and neglect those things that the impiety of the Christians has cultivated, their hospitality to strangers, their care of the graves, their holiness of life? We should earnestly seek all these things." "The godless Galileans," Julian went on, "see that the [pagan] priests neglect the poor, and then immediately take the opportunity for charity." Julian noted that the Christians did not limit their social work to their own communities but served the whole society. "For it is disgraceful, when there is not a beggar among the Jews, and when the godless Galileans support our poor as well as their own, that our people should be without our help." Julian not only exhorted his priests but himself moved to establish care for the poor and needy including for the first time the construction of alms-houses and hospitals. Julian thus attempted to imitate Christian social action in order to deprive the Christians of the effective power of their love for others.

Eusebius of Caesarea described not only care of the poor but of the sick. In his *The History of the Church*, he described responses to a plague from a letter by Dionysius of Alexandria.

> Most of our brother-Christians showed unbounded love and loyalty, never sparing themselves. . . . Heedless of the danger, they took charge of the sick, attending to their every need and ministering to them in Christ, and with them departed this life . . . for they were infected by others with the disease, drawing on themselves the sickness of their neighbors. . . . The heathen behaved in the very opposite way. At the first onset of the disease, they pushed the sufferers away and fled from their dearest, throwing them into the roads before they were dead

and treating unburied corpses as dirt, hoping thereby to avert
the spread and contagion of the fatal disease; . . .

Bolkestein notes that whereas in the East, including Israel
and Egypt, the support of the poor, especially widows and
orphans, was characterized as the greatest responsibility, it
was nearly never mentioned or praised in pre-Christian
Greek and Roman culture. The Greco-Roman temples of the
classical age did not promote any sense of care for others. The
rich had no ethical responsibility to the poor. There were no
lack of admonitions to the rich, but the emphasis was that the
wealthy should acquire and use their fortunes in an honorable
manner, and not pride themselves on their wealth. That they
should give of their wealth to the poor was not asked of them.
That is, the philosophies of the elite focused on eudaemonism
and the Greco-Roman religions made little or no connection
with ethics. In this sense, Uhlhorn echoes the assessment of
Lactantius (c.240–c.320), "the Christian Cicero," who emphasized that the pre-Christian era had no "charity" in the sense
of love of the neighbor.

The worship of the Greco-Roman gods and, later by the time
of the Christian era, emperor worship and cults, were integral
to Roman public life and citizenship. The religious acts of the
offering of sacrifice, prayer, and dedications, essential aspects
of Roman religion, were characterized by the term *pietas*. *Pietas*
meant "duty" and did not carry the connotations of our modern term "piety." Religious activities took place at the shrines
of the particular deities and were the province of the profes-
sional priests associated with the shrines.

The Roman *cultus* was primarily directed to maintaining
peaceful relations with the gods, the *pax deorum*. Contributions
in money and goods to the priesthood and ritual performance
was consumed by cultic performances or held as assets for
times of catastrophe to expiate the gods. Cult ritual therefore

had an end in itself: maintaining good relations with the gods. When Tertullian stated that Christians give more on the streets than pagans in their temples, he was demarcating the Christian faith from the religions of Rome. Tertullian, Ambrose, and others claimed that their faith engaged and alleviated the needs of the culture whereas in Rome's religions all money flowed into the cult alone. In the Roman cults there was not divine worship in any communal sense; rather the cultic performances were a sort of spectator sport where, if interested, people could watch – in silence! – the priests. There were no divine mandates or ethical expectations, but rather a kind of contract between the divinity in question and the person or persons making the sacrifice and prayers; a striking of a bargain. Since it was not intended that the good will of the gods would be gained by ethical conduct, the Hellenistic-Roman forms of religion were not conducive to love of the neighbor.

The well-known Greco-Roman *liberalitas* (liberality) was an aristocratic virtue exercised toward friends and fellow-citizens, but not toward the needy. The responsibility of "noblesse oblige" that led to the construction of public works such as public baths and roads may have benefited more than the friends of the benefactor, but the motivation was fame, honor, and esteem. These achievements were then memorialized in monuments – not quite the children of immortality Diotima extolled in her speech to Socrates in the *Symposium*, but "stone children" would do if you were not a poet. Humanitarian works for the poor did not merit monuments and inscriptions. There were also the "bread and circuses" – state-supported distributions of grain and sports events both in Rome and the provinces. Uhlhorn sums up civic welfare, such as it was: "It was an offering brought to vanity, to avarice, or to policy; it was a ransom which wealth paid to poverty in order not to be disturbed by it."

Uhlhorn further argues: "The ethics of the Greeks and Romans did not advance beyond a more or less refined eudaimonism. The chief principle of action is always one's own benefit. Even with Plato it is not otherwise, a fact which makes us wonder how it is that in the case of this best representative of the ancient world a naked egoism so frequently comes to the fore." Aristotle, too, in speaking of friendship assumes a selfish basis for generosity. "For all this generosity and benevolence springs not from love, but from the reflection that such conduct is decorous and worthy of a noble man."

Uhlhorn's evaluation of the Greco-Roman understanding of love sounds remarkably like Nygren's description of eros. Indeed, in an article critical of Nygren's analysis, Lowell Streiker agrees. Nygren's description of eros "pretty well summarizes Plato's teaching of love as it is found in the stages-of-ascent account of the *Symposium* and the love-as-the-rewinging-of-grounded-souls palinode of the *Phaedrus*." "As characterized by Plato, love is not a divine experience, i.e., the gods have no need to love, for they lack nothing. Love, the desire for what one does not have and the 'upward' movement toward it, is exclusively a human activity." But Streiker goes on to argue that Plato does not reduce the love of another to selfishness, and that Platonic eros has a legitimate use within Christian theology, as is clear in the case of Augustine. "In his understanding of love, Augustine is at once with Plato. Philosophy is the search for happiness, a quest for the good. This search, both Augustine and Plato would agree, can never end in finite, sensible objects. It can only reach fruition in the Eternal. In this way, Eros is truly man's quest for God. And without this quest, the so-called way of God to man would remain a trivial and irrelevant doctrine."

Thus it is to Augustine that we next turn to see how he related apparently conflicting views of love.

Chapter 4

Caritas: The Augustinian Synthesis of Biblical Agape and Hellenistic Eros

The person in the West who more than any other synthesized the Hellenistic heritage of eros with the biblical proclamation of agape was St. Augustine (354–430). His intellectual and spiritual journey from pagan philosopher and rhetorician to Christian priest and then bishop entailed profound reflection and writing upon his Greco-Roman heritage and the religious options of his day. His writings – autobiographical reflection, biblical studies, polemical works against rival religions and perceived heresies, creative theologizing on major topics, his numerous sermons and writings on pastoral care, and his end of life revisions – are too vast to even list here. We can only note selected aspects of his contributions to the history of the idea of love, and hope readers will be stimulated to pursue further readings.

No other theologian has been as influential upon the West as Augustine. He marked the theological–spiritual course for the church up to the modern period. Biographically a person of pagan and Christian culture, and profoundly influenced by both Greco-Roman culture and biblical faith, Augustine is often the lightning rod for the perennial theological and philosophical controversies over whether Western Christianity is a cultural synthesis or a cultural syncretism of its double origin in Greek and biblical religious views. If Christianity is to be characterized as a religion of love, is it eros or agape, or is it both?

Nygren asserted that "Augustine's view of love has exercised by far the greatest influence in the whole history of the Christian idea of love.... Ever since his time the meaning of Christian love has generally been expressed in the categories he created, and even the emotional quality which it bears is largely due to him." Likewise, O'Donovan argues "Until more detailed research proves otherwise, we must make the supposition that Augustine is responsible not only for the currency of 'self-love' in the theology of the West but also for the predominance of the 'summary' [i.e., the two-fold commandment to love] in Western Christian ethics." Nygren, among others, attributes Augustine's influence not only to his genius but to his context of living "on the frontier of two separate religious worlds, those of Hellenistic Eros and primitive Christian Agape."

Aurelius Augustinus was born in Thagaste (in contemporary Algeria), a provincial bourgeois milieu. His father was a pagan and his mother, Monica, was a devout Christian. Augustine lived in a time of great political and social crisis. By the time of his death while bishop of Hippo Regius, a small North African seaport and Roman military post, the city was under siege by the Vandals. Aleric's Visigoths had pillaged Rome and shaken the Roman world to its foundations in 410, the symbolic date for the end of the Roman Empire in the West.

Augustine lived in an afflicted society that appeared to be rushing pell-mell toward disintegration. "Eternal Rome" was collapsing as it faced perpetual warfare with barbarian war bands in the north and the challenge of Persia in the east. Taxation skyrocketed to finance the military; the poor were victimized by horrendous inflation; and the rich sought refuge in unparalleled accumulations of property. To add insult to injury for the Christians, the charge arose that all these disasters were the consequence of the abandonment of the traditional gods of the empire. In response to this pagan charge, Augustine wrote his famous theology of history, *The City of God*.

Augustine's family, though not rich, was free and he was bright. His father, Patricius, a minor official, perceived that economic advancement was through a classical education, and thus he scraped together the means for Augustine to gain such an education with its emphasis upon rhetoric. Patricius' ambition for his son coupled with Augustine's intelligence (he has been compared to Plato and Aristotle!) led to prestigious positions as a teacher of rhetoric in Carthage (376–383), Rome (383–384), and then Milan (384) where he was appointed to the municipal chair of rhetoric with its potential of further rise in prestige and power. A Roman citizen, Augustine's mother-tongue was Latin; he also had a modest acquaintance with Greek. Hence his vocabulary for love consisted of the Latin terms *amor*, *caritas*, and *dilectio*. Petré notes that Augustine tends to use *caritas* and *dilectio* as equivalents of the Greek agape while *amor* retains more of the Platonic sense of eros. His astounding mastery of the Greek philosophers came from Latin translations, his engagement with the intellectual circles of Milan that were pervaded by Platonism, and his exposure to a Christianized Plotinianism through bishop Ambrose of Milan. Furthermore, various forms of "Platonism" had infused the intellectual culture of the day in which Augustine avidly participated.

His mother, Monica, however was convinced through a dream that in spite of Augustine's quest for academic advancement he would be converted to Christianity. She followed

Augustine relentlessly in pursuit of her vision of his conversion. Augustine himself seems to have realized that her devouring love had an element of "unspiritual desire" in it for in his *Confessions* he wrote: "She loved to have me with her, as is the way with mothers, but far more than most mothers." Monica's dream was realized when Augustine was converted to Christianity in 386, the year before her death.

The first decades of Augustine's personal life were marked by his ambition, achievement, and entering into a quasi-marital relationship with his concubine. Concubinage was viewed as a socially sanctioned alternative to marriage when class disparity between the partners precluded a legal marriage according to Roman law. The relationship began when Augustine was studying in Carthage at the age of 17. Little is known about his mistress. They had a son, Adeodatus ("Given by God"), and lived together for the next 17 years. Apparently Augustine's mother, among others, urged him to put his mistress aside and contract a legal marriage with a woman of his class in order to advance his career. Monica argued that once Augustine was legally married, and then was baptized, he would be cleansed of his old relationship. The lack of sources for these events has contributed to the scholarly controversies over them. Fifteen years later in his *Confessions*, Augustine wrote: "[M]y mistress being torn from my side as an impediment to my marriage, my heart, which clung to her, was racked, and wounded, and bleeding. And she went back to Africa, making a vow unto Thee [God] never to know another man, leaving me with my natural son with her." Unwilling to wait for the proposed legal marriage, Augustine, as he says, "a slave to lust," found another mistress. Yet even years later, the pain of separation was still raw: "Nor was that wound of mine as yet cured which had been caused by the separation from my former mistress, but after inflammation and most acute anguish it mortified, and the pain become numbed, but more desperate." Soon after the dismissal of his mistress he also suffered the loss by death of his mother, his son, and two of his closest friends. It has been suggested that the rending of these relationships contributed to his developing conviction that God's love is the only safe love.

Insight into Augustine's development is provided by his *Confessions*, written between 397 and 401, after becoming a priest. Augustine felt he had to assess himself, and he did this by interpreting his past life as it led to his conversion. The *Confessions* are Augustine's effort to find himself. His conversion alone was not enough to sustain him. He had to work through his emotions regarding the death of his mother, for example, and reached the conclusion that the idealized figure who had haunted his youth was finally just an ordinary person, a sinner like himself. Augustine could have cut himself off from his past – a not unusual reaction to a conversion experience. Instead he called on his memory to understand his present. He dealt specifically with his feelings in relation to his personal growth and the nature of human motivation. Hence his account of stealing a pear is his paradigm for the sinful human condition. One would think that a cosmopolitan person like Augustine could have come up with a more lurid example! But, as he noted, it was not the pear he wanted to enjoy, but rather "the theft for its own sake, and the sin." He "derived pleasure from the deed simply because it was forbidden." He recalled how in his pagan life he had enjoyed crying at the theater, but had no reaction to the news of his father's death. In his reflections Augustine set the tone that would permeate medieval culture and theology up to the Reformation period and in many respects up to today. That tone is introspection.

Introspective self-scrutiny, seen in the *Confessions*, reflects the soul's longing for God, a longing to return to its maker, a longing experienced as restlessness, a pressing sense that in all things there lies something beyond, something that calls to God. The sense of not being at home in the world, the sense of alienation is fundamental to Augustine. But of course it is not unique to him or to Christianity. It is the Hellenistic tension between the transient and the permanent, the temporal and the eternal. It is what Plato expressed in the longing to escape the shadows of the cave and enter the sunshine of the intelligible world. It is the goal of immortality expressed in Plato's *Symposium*. It is even more clearly expressed in the writings of Plotinus whose writings reflecting Plato and Aristotle influenced Augustine. Van Fleteren in his article, "Ascent of the Soul," notes that in antiquity "ascent of the soul proceeds from the sensible world to the interior self and then to God. This motif underlies most of Augustine's early works, and two of his three major works, *Confessiones* and *De Trinitate*." Before his conversion Augustine had immersed himself in Hellenistic philosophy, and toward the end of his life in his major work, *The City of God*, he affirmed that Platonists excelled all other philosophers in logic and ethics. He relates in his *Confessions* that he had achieved intellectual ascent to the top of the Platonic "ladder of love" and saw "that which is." But in Augustine the longing for and ascent to God is transposed from human restlessness to a response to God's love and condescension; it is, in the opening lines of the *Confessions*, the movement of the Holy Spirit in the human heart: "for you have formed us for yourself, and our hearts are restless till they find rest in you." Later in the *Confessions*, he notes the difference between Platonic ascent and Christian ascent. The former is drawn upward by that erotic gravitational force, itself unmoved, that we saw earlier in Aristotle, or the draw of the Beautiful as we saw in Diotima's speech in the *Symposium*. The latter ascent is made possible by God's prior descent in Christ. In a famous line in the *Confessions*, that echoes Aristotle's theory that bodies gravitate to their places due to their weight,

Augustine says "my weight is my love." His Christian twist on Aristotle is that God's gift of love inflames him and thus like fire he is borne upward.

Divine Providence had led Augustine, he says, to "certain books of the Platonists, translated from Greek into Latin. And therein I read, not indeed in the same words, but to the selfsame effect, ... that, in the beginning was the Word, and the Word was with God, and the Word was God." What Augustine did not find in the Platonists was "that the Word became flesh and lived among us" (John 1:14). For Augustine, the Incarnation makes possible human ascent to God. Salvation, then, is not a human achievement but the gift of God's love. The realization of the Platonic eros depends upon the gift of agape through God's Incarnation.

Augustine's pre-conversion search for philosophical certainty was aided by his discovery of Neoplatonism. Instead of the forces of good and evil, Neoplatonism spoke of being and nonbeing. In this schema, evil is seen as a defect, a lack of being. Persons are pulled downward or direct their attention downward away from being toward nonbeing, and therefore are not what they ought to be. But as attractive as this philosophy was intellectually for Augustine, he was unable to put it into practice. Neoplatonism showed him the good, but did not enable him to reach it. He wondered how Christian monks, who to him did not appear very bright, could control themselves, but he with all his publicly acclaimed brilliance could not. The strict early Christian sexual ethic remained a stumbling block to Augustine's conversion. Yet Platonic thought helped prepare him for acceptance of the gospel. It was, Augustine says, God's design that he read the Platonists before the Scriptures.

The other major influence was the church in the person of Ambrose of Milan, a brilliant rhetorician who had embraced Christianity and then been acclaimed bishop.

Ambrose exhibited in his own person to Augustine that he did not have to sacrifice his intellect to become a Christian. Ambrose's Platonic worldview and his use of allegory in interpreting Scripture overcame Augustine's view that the Bible was inferior literature to the Latin classics. A further impetus to conversion was the story recounted by his countryman, Ponticianus, of the conversion of two of his friends on reading Athanasius's *Life of St. Antony*.

In his *Confessions*, Augustine recounts his conversion as a highly emotional event. He withdrew into his garden and flung himself down under a fig tree weeping for release from the anger and judgment of God, and heard a child chanting "Take up and read; take up and read." Interpreting this as a divine command, he opened the Bible and read the first passage he saw, Romans 13:13–14: "Let us live honorably as in the day, not in reveling and drunkenness, not in debauchery and licentiousness, not in quarreling and jealousy. Instead, put on the Lord Jesus Christ, and make no provision for the flesh, to gratify its desires." Instantly his gloom and doubt vanished.

Augustine's contributions to Western theology and church history are legion. Most noteworthy is his grounding Christian faith in the concept of love. He attempted to subsume Christianity as a whole under the aspect of love, from the doctrine of the Trinity to service to the neighbor. The key biblical passage is 1 John 4:8: "God is love" (*Deus dilectio est*). In *On the Trinity*, Augustine introduces chapter 8 with the assertion that "he who loves his brother, loves God; because he loves love itself, which is of God, and is God." He continues:

> Embrace the love of God, and by love embrace God.... [B]egin from that which is nearest us,...our brother. And listen how greatly the Apostle John commends brotherly love:... " Beloved, let us love one another: for love is of God; and every one that loves is born of God, and knows God. He that loves

not, knows not God; for God is love." And this passage declares sufficiently and plainly, that this same brotherly love itself (for that is brotherly love by which we love each other) is set forth by so great authority, not only to be from God, but also to be God. When, therefore, we love our brother from love, we love our brother from God; neither can it be that we do not love above all else that same love by which we love our brother: whence it may be gathered that these two commandments cannot exist unless interchangeably. For since "God is love," he who loves love certainly loves God; but he must needs love love, who loves his brother.... [A]nd we love ourselves so much the more, the more we love God.

Augustine's point is that the first realization of love to God is authentic love to the neighbor. Christianity is purely and simply the religion of love. Again, that love is not an abstraction, a pursuit of an idea, but expresses itself in love for the needy as seen for example in Augustine's use of church property to support the poor and exhortations to end their misery. Augustine articulated this motif so powerfully that it became axiomatic for Roman Catholic and much of Protestant theology to affirm Christianity is a religion of love.

As noted earlier, Augustine used the Latin *caritas* for Christian love. *Caritas* is the word from which we get "charity." The English "charity," however is too weak to convey Augustine's sense of *caritas* as "grace," "favor," "love," and "benevolence." *Caritas* in Augustine's sense is primarily love to God made possible because God first loved humankind. Love to God is the central virtue; all other virtues are expressions of it. With this theological orientation Augustine is free from all legalistic ethics. Only love is enjoined upon the Christian; where love is, no other requirements are necessary. Hence, Augustine's famous ethical injunction: "Love God and do what you will." *Caritas* is the root of all that is good; its opposite, the root of all that is evil, is *cupiditas*, the word from which we get "cupidity" and also "Cupid," the Roman god of love. *Cupiditas* has the sense of passionate desire, lust and wrongful appetite. Both *caritas* and *cupiditas* are terms for love. The difference between them is that *caritas* is directed to the sole true and real possibility for happiness, God; whereas *cupiditas* is (mis)directed toward things assumed to provide happiness but which are only transient. Both terms refer to "love" but are polar opposites – *caritas* ascends to God, Being itself; and *cupiditas* descends to inferior beings and then in its continual descent it reaches nothingness, nonbeing. Augustine's fundamental assumption – gained from his acquaintance with Neoplatonism – is that all love is acquisitive or an appetite. That is, persons desire what they believe will fulfill them. In short, Augustine perceives that the eudaemonism – the drive for self-fulfillment – of ancient philosophy has apologetic value. That is, the pagan question of how one may attain happiness is answered by the gospel proclamation that God's love is an imperishable gift. Everyone wants to be happy. By linking love closely to the desire for happiness, Augustine finds it possible to regard love as the most elementary of all manifestations of human life. There is no one who does not seek his or her happiness. For Augustine this is synonymous with the claim that there is no one who does not love; and that a person "is" what he or she loves. Here is the foundation for both the theology of ordered love that will develop in medieval scholasticism and the drive to union with God expressed by medieval mystics.

Equally important for Augustine is the awareness that no one is truly happy who lives in fear of losing the object or source of happiness. Once again, he sees the answer to the crisis of philosophical and existential anxiety in the gospel that *caritas* will not fail because it is God's grasp of the person rather than vice-versa. In this regard Harrison notes that one of Augustine's favorite texts is Romans 5:5: "God's love has been poured into our hearts through the Holy Spirit that has been given to us.''

Anything may be perceived as an object of good *for me* – thus even in evil the person loves nothing other than what he or she thinks is his or her good. In *The City of God*, Augustine writes:

> When the miser prefers his gold to justice, it is through no fault of the gold, but of the man; and so with every created thing. For though it be good, it may be loved with an evil as well as with a good love: it is loved rightly when it is loved ordinately; evilly when inordinately. It is this which some one has briefly said in these verses in praise of the Creator: ''These are Thine, they are good, because thou art good who did create them. There is in them nothing of ours, unless the sin we commit when we forget the order of things, and instead of Thee love that which Thou hast made.''

The fact that persons neglect the order of creation is due to the fall and sin, not the Creator. Creatures, being incomplete due to fall, always desire their completeness. Thus, to Augustine, self-love and the love of God must coincide. Persons always seek their own happiness, their own good; self-love seeks what is good for the self. If that good is sought in the creation rather than the Creator, it is self-deception, delusional. That love is inordinate, that is, disordered love. Only by loving God may we truly learn to love ourselves. We shall see that this is also the point made centuries later by Bernard of Clairvaux. In *On the Trinity*, Augustine states: ''The man who knows how to love himself, loves God; while the man who does not love God, though he retains the love of self which belongs to his nature, may yet properly be said to hate himself, when he does what is contrary to his own good. . . . It is therefore a fearful delusion, by which, though all men desire their own advantage, so many do what only works their ruin.''

This leads to consideration of the opposition between loves, between *caritas* and *cupiditas*. *Cupiditas* is sin because it is misdirected or disordered love; it is love directed to inferior objects which can never fulfill us; it is curved down toward the earth rather than upward toward God. God is above us, and thus we are to direct our love upward toward the good that is God. Earthly goods confuse us, and drag our love downwards toward them. *Cupiditas* then is the search for the good, which while good, is nevertheless incapable of providing final satisfaction. The difference between *caritas* and *cupiditas* is not the way love is expressed but the object of the love. *Caritas* is directed to the ultimate; *cupiditas* mistakes the penultimate for the ultimate. Here again we see the influence of Neoplatonism with its view that humans are incomplete and that therefore all human desires and strivings are directed to the attainment and possession of goods and values to overcome the recognized lack of being and therefore to perfect oneself. Being itself is the highest good; to turn away from the highest good, from Being, is to turn toward non-being. Augustine was thus using Hellenistic philosophy to express to his audience the biblical view that sin is not just breaking rules or laws but breaking relationships by turning away from God and the neighbor, breaking the chain of being. Since only God is the highest good, the immutable good, only God can give persons complete fulfillment. When love is directed to lower goods in the search for fulfillment it then becomes idolatrous, it mistakes the creature for the Creator; by loving perishable goods, sin is a turn or perversion toward privation and death. In his *Enchiridion* Augustine concludes: "[L]ust [*cupiditas*] diminishes as love [*caritas*] grows, till the latter grows to such a height that it can grow no higher here. For 'greater love hath no man than this, that a man lay down his life for his friends' [John 15:13]. Who then can tell how great love shall be in the future world, where there shall be no lust for it to restrain and conquer?

For that will be the perfection of health when there shall be no struggle with death."

The distinction between true and false love raises the question of Augustine's understanding of the creation. He rejected Manichaeism, an attractive rival religion of his day, with its radical dualism of the opposition of good and evil, spirit and matter that led to denigration of the material world. Augustine affirmed the goodness of creation because it is God's creation. Hence love of the creation is not in itself sin if this love is rightly understood. He clarified this by making a distinction between enjoyment (*frui*) and use (*uti*). *Frui* is the love that "enjoys" its object, whereas *uti* is the love that "uses" its object. The analogy Augustine used to illustrate this distinction is that of a voyage to our homeland. The ship is "used" as a means to get us to our home that we "enjoy." The ever-present temptation is that the voyage may so appeal to us that we forget home and enjoy the trip to the extent that it becomes an end in itself. The distinction between the love that "uses" and the love that "enjoys" raises another question that is more fraught for contemporary life than it was for Augustine: ecology. Certainly Augustine cannot be indicted for modern ecological destruction, but ideas such as the lesser goods of creation are for "use" not "enjoyment" do have consequences. When the right attitude to the world is to "use" it as a means to ascend to God, there may arise a "forgetfulness" of the goodness of creation and the world may lose its meaning as God's world. It may be argued that that was not Augustine's intention for he himself had vigorously rejected the dualistic anti-materialism of Manichaeism. His intent, briefly stated, appears in *On Christian Doctrine*: "[T]he whole temporal dispensation was made by divine Providence for our salvation. We should use it, not with an abiding but with a transitory love and delight . . . so that we love those things by which we are carried along for the sake of that toward which we are carried." Burnaby in his essay "*Amor* in St. Augustine" elaborates: "What Augustine frankly and thankfully recognizes is that God's goodness has so ordered his creation that the life which gives itself in love to God and neighbor is not and never can be a life lost. 'When you love him, you will be where your being is secure (*ibi eris, ubi non peris*).' " Rist (*Augustine*) writes: "Augustinian grace has come to perform the role of Platonic eros; the difference is that grace is unambiguously divine, no mere *daimon*, but the Holy Spirit; and the fact that love is God entails that it is omnipresent."

The earthly city is not the true home of the Christian, but rather the vehicle ("the ship") for our travel to our true home in the heavenly city. The world, our earthly city, is given as a means and vehicle for our return to God; it is to be used not enjoyed. The world, if enjoyed, drags us down and away from God. In *The City of God*, Augustine wrote: "Accordingly, two cities have been formed by two loves: the earthly by the love of self, even to the contempt of God; the heavenly by the love of God, even to the contempt of self. The former, in a word, glories in itself, the latter in the Lord." According to Daniel Day Williams, Augustine has bought into the Platonic metaphysic of a hierarchy of being with Being itself (the Highest Good) as immutable as well as absolute. The consequence is to relegate all other being to various positions in the great chain of being, characterized by transience and incompleteness. Since love of God is love of the immutable, every other love has a lesser place in Augustine's system of values. The issue in the succeeding history of Western Christendom became whether this disjuncture is spiritualized toward an ascetic otherworldliness or understood as the critical perspective for life in this world. One major aspect of the Augustinian heritage was an emphasis upon Christians as pilgrims in an alien land. In Augustine we find the themes of pilgrimage and alienation that become so influential in Western Christendom and culture. The motif of ascent to God will be illustrated in art and literature by images of the ladder to heaven. To be sure, Augustine emphasized that human ascent to God depends first of all upon God's descent to humankind; the descent of Christ enables human ascent to God.

D. W. Robertson concisely summarizes Augustine's contribution:

> At the heart of medieval Christianity is the doctrine of Charity.... Since this doctrine has extremely broad implications, it cannot be expressed satisfactorily in a few words, but for convenience we may use the classic formulation included in the *De doctrina Christiana* of St. Augustine: "Charity is called the movement of the soul to the enjoyment of God for his own sake, and that of the neighbor for the sake of God; cupidity on the other hand is the movement of soul to the enjoyment of self and the neighbor and whatever pleases the body not for the sake of God." The opposite of Charity, as St. Augustine describes it is cupidity, the love of any creature, including one's self, for its own sake. These two loves, Charity and cupidity, are the two poles of medieval Christian scale of values. For St. Augustine and for his successors among medieval exegetes, the whole aim of Scripture is to promote Charity and to condemn cupidity....

Chapter 5

Love and the Individual: Abelard and Bernard

After Augustine, Western life and culture entered a period of centuries of nearly unremitting struggle for survival and the development of a feudal, warrior culture. As if striving for daily bread were not a sufficient hardship, there were also the internal conflicts among the rulers themselves as well as against external terrors such as Viking and Magyar incursions. During this period up to the rise of cathedral schools and then fledgling universities in the twelfth century, there appear few records in either prose or poetry that could assist us in exploring the concept of love. What was characterized as love largely had political and communal reference such as alliances, the deference of vassals, and the bonds of monastic brotherhood. Love was understood mainly as an impersonal benevolence. Hamm reflects on this relative silence about the significance of love, saying that the rich emotional, philosophical, theological, and mystical expressions of love in classical pagan and Christian writers disappeared by the early sixth century. The cultural foundations of classical Mediterranean life, Hamm argues, were eroded especially in the Frankish kingdom by temporal and spatial distance.

Dinzelbacher also notes the paucity of poetry and writings on love before the High Middle Ages. If people reflected about love – as must certainly have been the case – they left few written records of their thoughts. Of course sexuality in all its expressions was not without witness for the penitential books from the seventh century on provide detailed proscriptions and norms. The sphere of earthly love, the erotic, was treated by the clergy only as a culpable realm; all too often presenting profane love as the wellspring of all evils and misfortunes. These guides for confessors on sin and penance perpetuated the suspicion of marriage and sexual relations promoted in the early church, and the elevation of virginity found in the writings of Augustine and Jerome. Of these two church fathers, Augustine was the more moderate, but both were critical of the writing of their contemporary Christian, Jovinian, who claimed marriage and virginity were equal goods. Jerome in particular is famous, or infamous as the case may be, for amplifying his anti-matrimonial views into misogynism.

In his tract, *The Excellence of Marriage*, Augustine wrote that marital intercourse is not sinful when the intent is procreation: "When it is for the purpose of satisfying sensuality, but still with one's spouse, because there is marital fidelity it is a venial sin. Adultery or fornication, however, is a mortal sin. For this reason abstinence from all sexual union is better even than marital intercourse performed for the sake of procreating." So much for Augustine's pre-conversion "joy of sex!"

Augustine, of course, was not alone in bequeathing this kind of double-think about sexual relations to the West. The church fathers of the second to fifth centuries all privileged virginity and justified sexual relations in marriage by procreation. On the one hand, the Genesis 1:26 ff. creation account states that Adam and Eve are told by God: "Be fruitful and multiply." On the other hand, in Genesis 4:1 f, "the man knew his wife Eve, and she conceived and bore Cain." Since the second account is after the fall and expulsion from Eden, some of the early church fathers viewed sexuality as a consequence of sin or at least a development simultaneous with the fall. Further weight was added by Paul's views in 1 Corinthians 7: "It is well for a man not to touch a woman" (7:1); "it is well for them [unmarried and widows] to remain unmarried" (7:8); but on the other hand "it is better to marry than to be aflame with passion" (7:9). Marriage is not a sin (7:28 & 36), but refraining from marriage is better (7:38). Paul's views were formed in light of his expectation of the imminent end of the world (7:26–31). But Paul's "situational ethic" of sexual relations was missed by the early and medieval church which no longer lived in Paul's context, and thus his contextual reflection became a normative devaluation of sexuality. The linking of sin and sexuality – original sin now becoming the first sexually transmitted disease – with the concomitant effort to remove *eros* from sexual relations initiated a long fateful history. The pathological fear of the feminine that surfaced in church fathers such as Jerome with its denigration of women continues into the modern period. It also contributed to Mariology by positing that the mother of Jesus had to be free of the stain of *eros* and mortality (dogma of the Immaculate Conception, 1854), and the prohibition of priesthood to women. The theological suspicion of women was tempered by the sixteenth-century Reformation revaluation of sexuality and marriage, but continued in Roman Catholicism into the modern period as evident by Pope Pius XI's dependence upon Augustine in his encyclical "On Chaste Marriage" (1930).

It would seem that with this tradition that reduced women to the roles of procreation and "remedy" within marriage for the "flames of passion" the human face of love would be permanently covered with the veil of shame. Nevertheless, sometime around the eleventh to twelfth centuries there is a rediscovery of the pluriformity of love – the love of Christ extolled in the devotional writings of the mystics that included erotic overtones; love between friends as related in collections of letters; love between the sexes as praised in the poetry and song of troubadour literature; love as romance, pain, and exploitation in the Goliard songs; love as erotic quest in the legends of Arthur and the myths of chivalry. In short, something new occurred in the expressions of love. The "new" may be related to what has been called the "birth of the individual." It is difficult to provide a precise definition and dating for this shift in consciousness. Morris, points to a scholarly consensus that an "increased vitality" and "a new respect for man and human possibilities" arose in this period. The earlier medieval view of God had perceived Christ less as the loving and suffering God than as the kingly judge *à la* medieval rulers. Christ is represented on the cross as "Christus rex," Christ the king, regally clothed and crowned looking out over his kingdom. Anselm of Canterbury (1033–1109), the "father of scholasticism," is significant in the history of theology for his theory of the atonement that shifted the focus from Satan's claim on humankind to the satisfaction of God's justice. Yet, even with this perspective, there remains in Anselm an earlier medieval emphasis upon the maintenance of God's honor and justice. God remains the cosmic model of the earthly experience of feudal barons and kings who ruled by fear and power. By the next generation, Anselm's impersonal-legal tradition, with its emphasis upon satisfying God's honor, shifted to an emphasis upon the saving love of the human Christ. God has given himself in order to recreate love. The crucifix now is rendered as the suffering servant stripped of regalia, a realistic human figure of humanity and pain. Likewise the earlier Romanesque and Gothic renderings of Mary and the child Jesus as stiff presentations of the "throne of wisdom," with Jesus, the little man, holding an orb, gave way to a Madonna image portraying a human mother and child, who nestle together or kiss one another. There is a new intimacy, a more intensive bodily closeness. Bernard of Clairvaux (1090–1153) epitomized this shift in his "Sermon 20" in his collection *On the Song of Songs*: The humanity of God intended to "draw the affections of carnal men, who could only love carnally, to a salutary love of His Flesh, and then on to a spiritual love."

The "humanism" of the period was marked by two developments: fluency in reading and writing Latin, and growing regard for the humanity of persons. The facility to verbalize thoughts and feelings was essential to reflection upon self, others, and the environment of one's life. Some six centuries after Augustine's *Confessions*, there is once again the exploration of inwardness, introspection, and feelings in autobiographical literature and letters. The interest, indeed fascination, with personal character and development present in Augustine and revived in the twelfth century distinguishes Western literature from the classical Greek myths. Morris notes that "Greek tragedy was a drama of circumstance, whereas the Western tragedy is essentially a drama of character." To put this in the terms for love we have already discussed: Greek Eros is a *daemon*, a force beyond oneself; whereas the biblical *agape* is relational. To cite Morris again: "The personal character of Oedipus is really irrelevant to his misfortunes, which were decreed by fate irrespective of his own desires. Conversely, the tragedies of Shakespeare turn on the flaw in the hero's own character." Thus in *Julius Caesar*, we read: "The fault, dear Brutus, is not in our stars, but in ourselves."

The medieval discovery of the individual and its significance for conceptions of love occurred about the same time in theological and courtly literature. We shall look at the latter's expressions of love in the poetry of the troubadours in the next chapter. The former is exemplified in the conflicting lives and writings of Peter Abelard (1079–1142) and Bernard of Clairvaux (1090–1153). Each was a superb Latinist; and each was concerned with love. And while they shared the introspective individualism shaped by love that characterized the age, they were also bitter opponents. It may well be that the closest thing to concave is convex.

Abelard, born in Brittany of a knight named Berengar and his wife Lucia, both of whom later entered monastic life, was driven by his quest for learning, willing to forfeit his inheritance in search of his holy grail, knowledge. Abelard's exceptional brilliance was matched by his self-esteem. Both characteristics played significant roles in his life, much of which we know about through his autobiography, appropriately titled *The Story of My Misfortunes* (*Historia calamitatum*, thus also translatable as the "history of my calamities"!), ostensibly written to provide comfort to an unnamed friend going through his own difficulties. He studied with some of the most prominent philosophers and theologians of his day, but was often dismissive of their work. Nevertheless he did gain the teaching position of "Master" at the cathedral school of Notre Dame. It was here that he met Heloise, fell in love, clandestinely married, had a son, and was castrated by Heloise's angry uncle and guardian. We shall return to this major love story of the Middle Ages in a moment. But first a brief sketch of Abelard's life and work to set the stage for reflections on the influence upon him of the love of Heloise.

Abelard made numerous significant philosophical, theological, and ethical contributions – many of which, it seems, his contemporaries did not fully understand and thus, enhanced by his personality, he appeared as a threat to what they perceived to be the orthodox tradition. His first major theological work, an explication of the Trinity, *Theologia Summi Boni*, was condemned at the Synod of Soissons (1121) where he was forced to throw it on the fire with his own hand. By now his opponents included the formidable monastic mystics William of St. Thierry (c.1085–1148) and Bernard of Clairvaux, both of whom, ironically, wrote influential treatises on love of God and the neighbor. Bernard remains famous for his extensive sermon series on the Song of Songs, that most erotic book of the Bible. Abelard was condemned to eternal silence as a heretic at the Synod of Sens in 1140. His opponents were also disturbed by his, to them, erosion of morality by his work on ethics *Scito te ipsum* ("Know Thyself") that emphasized personal intention as the determinant of whether or not an act is sinful. According to Gurevich, that was "a principle that was new for that age" and reflects the emergence in Abelard of "a new type of individual." Acts themselves are morally indifferent; it is the intention behind them that makes them right or wrong. There is an echo here of Augustine's phrase, "love God and do what you will." The motif of love is equally present in Abelard's theology of salvation, that Weingart aptly titled *The Logic of Divine Love*. The essential God–human bond is love freely given by God. Sin breaks this relationship, but because God is love he re-creates fellowship with his creatures through the incarnation of love in Jesus Christ. The renewal and transformation of the person through divine love liberates the person from the rule of selfish love, *cupiditas*, and directs him or her toward an existence determined by selfless love, *caritas*. Salvation, then for Abelard, is "the logic of divine love." Weingart notes Abelard's unique conception of the uniting in love of persons and God. "[M]an is justified and sanctified by God in love, he is recreated by the infusion of love, he lives a life of love in the community of the faithful." In short, God's love is discovered and realized in human relationships; and that brings us to the love affair of Abelard and Heloise and its influence upon Abelard's theology.

Abelard himself records the story of his affair in his autobiography. He notes that not only was he inordinately proud of his intellectual abilities and learning, he also thought he cut a rather dashing figure with the ladies. With his characteristic modesty he wrote: "So distinguished was my name, and I possessed such advantages of youth and comeliness, that no matter what woman I might favour with my love, I dreaded rejection of none." In light of his position as Master in the Cathedral School of Notre Dame, he notes that he avoided "the foulness of prostitutes" and the noblewomen who attended the school. However, he soon noticed Heloise, the brilliant, young, and comely niece of Abelard's fellow canon, Fulbert, at the Cathedral of Notre Dame. Since Fulbert was her guardian, she lived in his lodgings. Heloise (c.1094–1164) was at this time about 20 years old; Abelard was in his mid-thirties. In Heloise's letters, collected in the volumes by Mews and Radice, it is clear that in her Abelard met his intellectual equal. Her writings exhibit an amazing conversance with the church fathers and classical authors, including the writings of Ovid. Inflamed with passion for her, Abelard set out to seduce her. He persuaded Fulbert to rent him a room in the canon's lodgings that were near the Cathedral. The arrangement included Abelard's promise to tutor her in philosophy and Greek. They soon proceeded to conjugate more than verbs and she became pregnant. Abelard recollected: "Under the pretext of study we spent our hours in the happiness of love, . . . No degree in love's progress was left untried by our passion, and if love itself could imagine any wonder as yet unknown, we discovered it." Abelard's attention was thus diverted, to the dismay and anger of his students, from philosophy and theology to poetry and love songs, which, he claimed, spread abroad and became the talk of Paris. Although no love poems from the time may be unequivocally attributed to Abelard, George Whicher in his *The Goliard Poets* includes some poems which may be the lost lyrics. One might be "Moonlight Sonata" that concludes:

> But O, how many are the changes
> Through which a lover's spirit ranges!

No ship that drifts
With anchor lost
Can match the shifts
Of hope and fear
Wherewith he's crossed:
The folk of Venus buy her service dear.

Heloise exulted in her pregnancy, but Abelard spirited her away to his sister in Brittany where their son was born. Heloise named him Astralabe, after the astronomer's instrument, perhaps in allusion to star-crossed love or heavenly bearings for their love. Fulbert, who had doted on his niece, was enraged when he discovered the affair and its consequence. Abelard offered marriage, provided "the thing could be kept secret, so that I might suffer no loss of reputation thereby." We might note that at this time clergy in minor orders such as Abelard were still in an ambiguous situation vis-à-vis marriage. It was not until the first Lateran Council in 1123 that celibacy of the major clergy was mandated. Furthermore, a number of significant theologians and some synods argued against mandatory celibacy all the way into the fifteenth century. Nevertheless, the consensus of the day was that professors remain celibate; also, marriage would have been a bar to a church career, the prime avenue for Abelard's advancement.

Heloise herself rejected the thought of marrying Abelard on the basis that it would disgrace him and impede if not ruin his career. She informs him of the hardships of married life. "Heloise bade me observe what were the conditions of honourable wedlock.... What man, intent on his religious or philosophical meditations, can possibly endure the whining of children, ... or the noisy confusion of family life? Who can endure the continual untidiness of children?" Heloise asserted "it would be far sweeter for her to be called my mistress than to be known as my wife; . . . In such case, she said, love alone would hold me to her, and the strength of the marriage chain would not constrain us." After the birth of Astralabe, who was left with Abelard's sister, the couple returned to Paris, were secretly married with but a few friends and Fulbert present.

Their plan was to live separately in order to conceal the marriage. Fulbert, however, could not reconcile himself to their relationship and began to abuse Heloise. Abelard then sent her to a nunnery for her protection. Fulbert interpreted this as Abelard's effort to rid himself of Heloise by forcing her to become a nun. Incensed, Fulbert and some relatives burst in upon Abelard during the night while he slept. "There they had vengeance upon me with a most cruel and most shameful punishment, . . . for they cut off those parts of my body with which I had done that which was the cause of their sorrow." Finding himself permanently celibate, Abelard became a monk and later a priest. The love affair of Abelard and Heloise was immortalized in literature by Jean de Meun in his great thirteenth-century allegory of courtly love and satire on women and marriage, *The Romance of the Rose*.

Heloise herself took monastic vows and eventually became an abbess, but as we learn from her letters to Abelard written after his *Historia Calamitatum* her passionate love had not abated:

> God knows, I sought nothing in you except you yourself; simply you, not lusting for what was yours. I expected no bonds of marriage, no dowry of any kind, not any pleasures or wishes of my own, but I sought to fulfill yours, as you yourself know. . . . I preferred love to marriage, freedom to chains. I call God as my witness, that if Augustus, presiding over the whole world, saw fit to honor me with marriage and confirmed the whole world on me to possess for ever, it would seem dearer and more honorable for me to be called your prostitute (*meretrix*) than his empress (*imperatrix*).

Unfettered friendship, closeness to Abelard, meant more to Heloise than any slander directed to her as she declared her love for him to be completely pure. Heloise expresses a "disinterested love" for Abelard comparable to his expression of God's love for humankind. Heloise's refusal to color her freely given love by obligation through marriage is echoed by Richard de Fournival (1201–1260) in his "Advice on Love": "[M]arried love is like a debt which one must pay, while the love of which I speak is a kind of grace freely bestowed. Although it is a mark of good manners to pay what one owes, still there is no more delightful love than that born of the gratuitous favor of an artless, ingenuous heart." Mews states: "Heloise's ideal of love integrated three normally distinct concepts: *amor*, the passion or subjective experience of love; *dilectio*, an act of choice by which one consciously decided to love another person; and *amicitia*, or friendship." In one of her early letters, she reflects on "what love is or what it can be by analogy with our behavior and concerns, that which above all forms friendships, and once considered, leads to repaying you with the exchange of love and obeying you in everything."

Heloise's obedience, however, cost her dearly. She did become an influential nun and abbess, learnedly questioning and conversing about liturgy, hymnody, and theology while also meeting and corresponding with major figures of her day such as Bernard of Clairvaux and Peter the Venerable (c. 1092–1156), Abbot of Cluny. But she never overcame her love of Abelard and the pain of separation. From the cloister she wrote to him that it was his command, "not love of God which made me take the veil." She cannot forget their past pleasures. "Wherever I turn they are always there before my eyes, bringing with them awakened longings and fantasies which will not even let me sleep. Even during the celebration of the Mass, when our prayers should be purer, lewd visions of those pleasures take such a hold upon my unhappy soul that my thoughts are on their wantonness instead of on prayers.''

The news of Abelard's death reached Heloise in a letter from Peter the Venerable who extolled Abelard's faith, humility in persecution, devotion, and knowledge. Peter, following Abelard's request, brought Abelard's body to the Paraclete cloister which Abelard had founded and where Heloise had become abbess. At Heloise's request, Peter also provided a written absolution of Abelard to be placed over his tomb. She also requested Peter to help her son Astralabe gain a benefice in one of the cathedrals. Little is known of what became of Astralabe, who was rarely mentioned in the correspondence of Abelard and Heloise. Heloise herself died in 1163 or 1164, perhaps as romantics like to think, at the same age that Abelard died, 63. She was buried alongside Abelard in the abbey church. Their bodies were moved over the centuries until in the nineteenth century they were interred together in the famous Père Lachaise cemetery in Paris where to this day flowers are occasionally placed beside their effigies.

The extent to which Heloise may have influenced Abelard's theology will remain speculative without further textual evidence. In light of Heloise's arguments against marriage, she may well have influenced Abelard's formulation of an ethic of intention. As she wrote to him: "It is not the deed but the intention of the doer which makes the crime, and justice should weigh not what was done but the spirit in which it is done." In an age that prized the authority of tradition, they boldly questioned the institutions of marriage and church, perceiving internal conflicts as well as external oppression. It is hard to imagine Abelard's re-thinking of the classical theories of the atonement, shifting attention from the satisfaction of God's wrath and justice to God's unlimited love without hearing echoes of Heloise's professions of love: "I never sought anything in you except yourself." Indeed,

Clanchy argues that Heloise was Abelard's "inspiration...as she can be shown to have expressed these ideas before he did." Clanchy continues: "The hypothesis that Heloise set Abelard's agenda in theology helps to explain why he addressed his final confession of faith to her, and not to the persecutors at Sens and in Rome who were demanding it.... In embracing Christ, Abelard was also embracing Heloise, as the document addresses her as: 'now dearest in Christ'."

The passionate romance of Heloise and Abelard has attracted major attention in our own day with a spate of scholarly studies and biographical works. In their own day and the following centuries, however, their story received far less attention. Jean de Meun's satirical continuation of the *Romance of the Rose* (c.1280) uses them to illustrate the dangers and burdens of marriage. But Dante (1265–1321), himself inspired by his Beatrice, does not mention them. Petrarch (1304–1374), however, showed more interest in them, especially Heloise. Burge comments that Petrarch was "besotted" by her. "Petrarch has seen Heloise's full range: she is by turns intelligent, sexy, stylish, and faithful. This is a combination that has always made scholars fall for her." Radice in her "Introduction" to the correspondence suggests that the contemporary ideal of courtly love overshadowed the Heloise–Abelard story. In contrast to the troubadours' celebration of the "chase" of the unattainable lady, the sensuous physical consummation and courageous bearing of their separation place Abelard and Heloise outside the "mannered and artificial" "romances of chivalry."

Abelard's theology clearly ruffled the feathers of his opponents. Chief among them was Bernard of Clairvaux, monastic reformer and mystic theologian, self-appointed judge, jury, and prosecutor of Abelard. What galled Bernard was not Abelard's love affair with Heloise but rather Abelard's use of dialectical reason to analyze and express the fundamental doctrines of the faith. Bernard's point of view, echoing that of Gregory the Great (d. 604), is that love, not reason, is the knowing faculty of the human mind (*"Amor ipse intellectus est,"* "love itself is a form of knowing"). By "knowing" the mystic means more than acquisition of information and concepts, but rather awareness, experiential union, in the sense that the Hebrew Bible uses "knowing" for sexual intercourse. Love is the affective ascent to union with God. The person who does not love does not know God because God is love. It seems that Bernard and Abelard were closer than either thought.

Born into a noble family, Bernard by the age of 22 persuaded 30 other young noblemen, including his brothers, to join the Benedictine renewal movement that had recently developed into an order in its own right, the Cistercians (named after its foundation in Citeaux). The rigor of the Cistercian reform had brought the new community to the edge of extinction when Bernard arrived. His influence became so strong that the Order was at times referred to as the "Bernardines." In 1115 he became the founding abbot at Clairvaux; by the time of his death there were some 340 Cistercian cloisters throughout Europe. Bernard has been called the "uncrowned ruler of Europe" because of his multifaceted influence upon the election of popes, politics of kings, preaching of crusades, reforms of the church, and pursuit of heretics. Above all, however, it was Bernard's promotion of a mystical love piety that secured his fame then and now. Thus Dante presented Bernard in the *Divine Comedy* as the representative of mystic contemplation who leads him to the Virgin Mary in Paradise.

Astell in her study, *The Song of Songs in the Middle Ages*, provides a summary of modern research on the Cistercians that provides insight into the fascination with this erotic poem and Bernard's famous sermons on it written for his community. The men who entered the new Cistercian communities were to a great extent from the noble class who entered the religious life as adults. "Many of them had been married or had had sexual experiences. . . . Their ranks included former troubadours, and evidence suggests that the Cistercian recruits were familiar with the popular songs of secular love literature." Allen makes the same point, adding that some of the recruits to the newer monastic orders "were even troubadours and trouvères. The popularity of Ovid, the worldly experience of these religious, and the church's belief that secular love was purely and simply sexual produced a literature of the cloister that was by no means strictly spiritual; indeed, Leo Pollmann suggests that obscene texts may have been acceptable precisely because they reinforced commonly held ideas about the nature of secular love." The context, Astell notes, may help understand the perpetual problem in studies of Bernard: "the apparent contradiction between his matter (spiritual love) and his manner of conveying it (the *amor* of the Song)." While Freudians may view such imagery in terms of "obsessive sexual repression," medievalists tend toward correlating Bernard's imagery to "the psychological needs and experiences of his audience," the goal being "the soul's mystical marriage with the Word."

Bernard's tremendous spiritual influence resided not only in the power of his personality but also in the readiness of his age to look inward, a readiness that also informed and received Anselm of Canterbury's emphasis upon "faith in search of understanding" (*fides quaerens intellectum*) and Abelard's emphasis upon intention. Bernard's extensive writings include treatises, letters, and sermons; the latter taking form as biblical-liturgical commentaries. His masterpiece, 86 sermons on the Song of Songs, composed over a period of about 20 years up to his death, comments on about a third of the book. This work and his *On Loving God* set forth the mystical path of love which leads to a loving union with Jesus, the Divine Bridegroom. The human fall into sin profoundly damaged the divine "image and likeness" in which humankind was created. Bernard therefore posited that the return to God occurred in stages of love that rose from self-love to spiritual love of God initiated by "the carnal love" of Christ, i.e., the Incarnation. Self-love is seen here as natural to creation, but this *eros* can be satisfied only in God.

Evans, in her study *The Mind of St. Bernard of Clairvaux*, comments that "the *cupiditas* or desire which underlies all natural appetites has been sustained and directed and subordinated by *caritas*, until all its inferior tendencies are gone and desire has become pure love." Evans also notes that much of the writing on love in the twelfth century spoke of progress, development, ascent of the soul: "Like the ladder of humility, the ladder of love is a step-by-step progression to a perfection to be realized only in the life to come. Love is a mountain to be climbed." And that climb is possible through the human cooperation with divine grace.

The motif of an ascent of love toward its true goal of union with God is reminiscent of Augustine's distinction of use and enjoyment in the imagery of travel to our homeland during which we use the ship as means toward our future enjoyment of home. At best, then, Bernard perpetuates an ambiguity toward creation, the temporal order of things, and erotic sexual relationships.

Dinzelbacher in his essay on the discovery of love in the High Middle Ages notes that at the same time as Abelard there is a renewed clerical interest in love. Bernard of Clairvaux exemplifies a new theological and spiritual programme with his "On the Necessity to Love God." So did his contemporaries William of St. Thierry ("On the Nature and Dignity of Love"), Aelred of Rielvaux ("The Mirror of Love"), Hugh of St. Victor ("On the Praise of Love"), Richard of St. Victor ("On the Degrees of Love"), among others. These treatises on Christian love correspond to the increasing number of commentaries on the Song of Songs. More exegetes now turned to this biblical book than had in the entire previous thousand years. The most famous of these commentaries is Bernard's sermons on the Song of Songs which were incorporated into the Cistercian liturgy.

Bernard differed from the Anselm's exposition of the Incarnation (*Cur Deus homo*) with its feudal orientation to the satisfaction of God's honor. For Bernard the primary motive for God becoming a human is not the rectification of the violated order of creation, but love for fallen humankind. So Bernard could write: "In the Scripture I have read that God is love, but never that he is honor and dignity." "Honor" and "dignity," the two central concepts of feudal thought and society, appear to Bernard as dissolved in love. God has given himself to pay for human sin, in order to gain the love of humankind. In turn, God's love enables humankind to concentrate upon the saving love of the human Christ and thus move step by step toward spiritual love. The consequent ascent to God begins with the person loving him or herself; next loving God in terms of personal self-interest; and on the third and fourth levels, attaining pure love of God, now loving him or herself only through God. The love of the Christ of the Eucharist is replaced by love of the historical person Jesus.

Bernard broke with the older commentaries on the Song of Songs with their allegorical identification of the bride with the church, and instead identified the bride with the human soul. In Sermon 83, Bernard wrote: "Now the Bridegroom is not only loving; he is love. Is he honor too? Some maintain that he is, but I have not read it. . . . Honor which is not inspired by love is not honor but flattery. Honor and glory belong to God alone, but God will receive neither if they are not sweetened with the honey of love. . . . [W]hen God loves, he desires nothing but to be loved, since he loves us for no other reason than to be loved, for he knows that those who love him are blessed in their very love." For Bernard, the God who is love displaces the feudal image of God who demands honor and judges the world. The mysticism of love and suffering began with the new consciousness of the historicity of Jesus and his passion. These elements of love and suffering also found expression in the growing cult of the sacred heart of Jesus and the honoring of Mary as an earthly maiden. Love alone enables humans to emulate God because the divine attributes of power and wisdom are beyond human capacities.

About this same time period a new form of mysticism arose. According to McGinn, *The Flowering of Mysticism* that began around 1200 "marked a major turning point in the mysticism of Western Christianity." Women played a major role in the new forms of mysticism expressed among the Beguines and the Mendicants with their emphasis upon ecstatic experience and conceptions of union with God. McGinn also makes the point that these women mystics of the first half of the thirteenth century utilized and transposed the courtly love poetry of the *trouvères*, the northern minstrels, in their mystical writings. That brings us to our next chapter, an exploration of the ideas of love expressed by troubadours and women mystics.

Chapter 6

Mystics and Troubadours

While Bernard was extolling the love of God that ultimately leads to love of oneself for the sake of God, poets were extolling the love of woman for the ennoblement of man. What is notable from the twelfth century on is that Christian theological and mystical conceptions of love on the one hand and secular courtly love on the other hand intertwine. We can see this development in relation to medieval interpretations of the relationship of the bridegroom and bride in the Song of Songs. In the early church through the early Middle Ages, their relationship was allegorized with Christ as bridegroom and the church as the bride. With the discovery of the individual in the twelfth century, Bernard makes the bold move of shifting the interpretation of the bride from the church to the individual soul, an interpretive move assisted by the fact that soul in Latin is a feminine noun (*anima*). By the next generation, especially among Christian women mystics, the bride is the mystic herself and the bridegroom is Christ or the Trinity. In addition, the writings of the women mystics described this relationship with the erotic themes of troubadour writings!

Also, by this time Ovid's works on love along with his other works became so often studied that the period is characterized as the "*aetas Ovidiana*," the age of Ovid's works. In this age of Ovidian revival, his *Ars amatoria*, the *Art of Love*, became especially well known. It was adapted to the medieval feudal society and thus circulated in the vernaculars as well as Latin. It is not surprising that in an age that revered literary authorities, Ovid's writings provided models not only for creative writing but especially for the age's new fascination with human love. As McCarthy notes, echoes of Ovid are in Abelard's account of his affair with Heloise, and in the imaginative works of Andreas Capellanus, Guillaume de Lorris, Geoffrey Chaucer, and John Gower. Allen in his *The Art of Love* details the medieval reception and transmission of Ovid's works noting that the major writers of the time "knew their Ovid as well as their Bible by heart." Giovanni Boccaccio's (1313–1375) *Decameron* utilized Ovid's love stories and praised them as a "holy book that showed how to kindle sacred fires of Venus in cold hearts." Chaucer (1343–1400) spoke of Ovid as "Venus's clerk" (i.e., priest). Francesco Petrarch (1304–1374) also knew Ovid, but condemned him as wanton. Thus Ovid's influence extended on into the Renaissance.

The parallel to Ovid among monastic writers was the erotic imagery of the Song of Songs. If this is the age of Ovid, it is also the age of the Song of Songs reaching its apogee in Bernard's extensive sermons on the text and the literary descriptions by women mystics – cloistered and non-cloistered – of their ecstatic experiences and raptures. The latter have long intrigued and puzzled their readers. Graphic images portray these saintly women in ways that depict them in an orgasm with an arrow through the heart. And their own writings provide erotic descriptions of their union with God. Markale provides a few examples. St. Gertrude (1256–1302): "My heart craves the kiss of your love, my soul thirsts for the most intimate embrace joining me to you." Mechtild von Magdeburg (1241–1299): "Lord, love me hard, love me long and often. I call you, burning with desire. Your burning love enflames me constantly. I am but a naked soul, and you, inside it, a richly adorned guest." Hadewijch of Antwerp (first half of thirteenth century): "My heart and my arteries, and all my limbs quivered and trembled with desire. I felt myself so violently and dreadfully tested it appeared that if I did not give satisfaction to my lover entirely, to know him, to taste him in every part of his body and if he did not respond to my desire, I would die of rage. . . . He came, handsome and sweet, . . . I approached him submissively . . . And he gave himself to me as he usually does, in the form of the sacrament. Then he came to me in person and took me in his arms and locked me in his arms. All my limbs felt this contact with his with equal intensity, following my heart, as I had desired. Thus externally, I was satisfied and quenched. . . . Following which, I remained merged with my lover until I had melted entirely within him in such a way as nothing was left of me." McGinn in *The Flowering of Mysticism* provides more examples of such erotic mystical writings by Mechtild, Hadewijch and others. McGinn notes that these writings may be described as "courtly mysticism" because of their close relation to the literary genre of courtly love. These women mystics with their focus on "bridal mysticism" have been called "the troubadours of God."

Northern European courtly lyrics go by the name *Minnesang*, literally "love song." The *Minnesang* theme relates the yearning of a knight for his lady (normally a married woman of higher class), and his offer of homage without reward but with hope of union with her. In his striving toward that ultimate goal, the knight encounters numerous obstacles he must overcome through self-renunciation and heroic deeds. McGinn's chapter on Hadewijch describes and analyses how "*Minne* is Hadewijch's all-embracing theme." "*Minne* brings God to the mystic and the mystic to God." Hadewijch used the erotic language of courtly love songs as the medium for perceiving the metaphysical within the physical realm. She and her mystical colleagues experienced that true love is rewarded with a radical renewal of one's being. The creative power of love they then compared to the creating power of God. At the same time, along with the Minnesingers and troubadours, these women mystics recognized that erotic bliss can be bound up with great pain, disappointment, and despair that plunges the lover into an abyss from which there seems to be no rescue. Finally, along with Bernard, there is the sense that mystical union is inexpressible. To cite McGinn again: "Love is meant to be explored and experienced in all its many moods and forms rather than defined and categorized. . . . Although *minne* [love] is mysterious for Hadewijch, it is absolutely necessary – the very meaning of existence. 'I will tell you without beating around the bush,' she says, 'be satisfied with nothing less than *minne*.' *Minne* is the air that she breathes: 'I have nothing else: I must live on *minne*.' "

Obviously the feudal imagery of the Christus Rex, the God of terrifying majesty, is giving way to the image of Jesus the Bridegroom. The new sensibility of feelings is evident in the increasing use of the heart as the symbol of love. The heart begins to complement and even displace the head as the site of the soul. It is the personal center in which the poet may keep his beloved; indeed lover and beloved may "exchange" hearts. McGinn refers to the woman mystic Lutgard of Aywières's (1182–1246) "major contribution to mystical piety – her emphasis on the bleeding heart of Christ." She and Jesus "exchange hearts." The "bleeding heart" piety soon became a phenomenon among other female mystics, especially St. Mechtild and St. Gertrude, and eventually developed into the Feast of the Sacred Heart when Pope Clement XIII authorized the Mass and Office of the Feast in 1765.

A number of scholars of these writings note that the radicality with which these poets developed their concept of love without any inhibitions, combining erotic and religious elements in Christian literature, still awaits more intensive research. Such writings have provoked various responses from spiritualizing denial to awe to jealousy. An example of the latter is the first poet laureate of Germany, Conrad Celtis (1459–1508). Celtis, author of *Amores* and a study of the tenth-century nun Roswitha of Gandersheim among other works, and who died of syphilis, expressed his chagrin that nuns could write better erotic verse than he.

The troubadour valorization of women had a variety of consequences ranging from mundane to profound. On the mundane level, de Rougemont notes that it is at this time that a radical change occurs in the game of chess. "Instead of the four kings which had dominated the game in its first form, a Lady (or Queen) was made to take precedence over all other pieces, save the King, and the latter was actually reduced to the smallest possibility of real action, even though he remained the final stake and the consecrated figure." Toward the more profound end of the spectrum, it is at this time that devotional and theological reflection on Mary, the mother of Jesus, intensified. De Rougemont argues that the development of Mariology was an effort to counter the powerful rise of courtly love and the cult of the idealized woman by co-opting courtly love as a defense measure. "Hence the repeated attempts from the beginning of the twelfth century onwards to institute a worship of the Virgin. It is from that time that Mary has generally received the title of *Regina coeli* [Queen of Heaven] . . . The monastic orders which were then being founded were retorts to the orders of chivalry. A monk was 'a Knight of Mary'. In 1140, at Lyons, the canons set up a Feast of the Immaculate Conception of Our Lady." The devotional use of the Hail Mary has eleventh-century roots and became common in the twelfth century. The teaching of Mary's immaculate conception – that Mary was conceived without sin – while having some patristic roots, was developed in eleventh-century England and introduced into France in the mid-twelfth century. Marian devotion and Mariology often were indistinguishable, and it is striking that the cult of the Virgin Mary coincides with the triumph of the Lady of courtly love – "Madonna" and "ma donna." Markale notes that both Mary and the Lady of the troubadours present salvation, the ascent to God, through the intermediary of the woman. Mary is "Our Lady" (Notre Dame) to whom sanctuaries are built. Boase notes that "between 1170 and 1270 the French built eighty cathedrals and nearly 500 churches of the cathedral class, most of which were dedicated to the Virgin Mary." She is the "Bonne Mère," the mother of all Christians, and thus each must share her with his or her siblings. Her mother role is jeopardized if her sexuality is raised and she is thought of amorously as "my lady," hence the emphasis upon her virginity. Markale sees the church's development of the cult of the Virgin Mary as the effort of a patriarchal clerical culture "to absorb feminist exaltation."

Mary's profane counterpart, the Lady of courtly poetry, is indeed my lady (*ma dame*, *ma donna*), also termed "my lord" (*midons*). The troubadour poetry of approaching the lady, gaining her favor, and winning her love is a "liturgy" analogous to that celebrated in the church in honor of Mary. Martin notes the influence here of classical mythology. "Venus and Cupid retain their traditional roles. But the religion of love in the courtly framework is often carried one step further in that, in more extreme cases, the lady is substituted for the goddess. In essence, it is a Christianization of a pagan religion. The courtly lady is adored as the Christian adores God. The lover is constantly seeking her grace, or her 'mercy'; at times he even prostrates himself before her in an attitude of worship.... On one level she assumes the role of lord in the feudal sense; on a higher level she becomes Lord in the religious sense."

Markale notes that courtly love set in motion a new art of loving and thereby a new art of living. To live is to love and vice-versa, and thereby the connection is made with the Christian tradition. So it could be remarked that the inversion of the Latin *Roma*, center of the medieval church, is *Amor*. The troubadour "service of love" develops on the basis of renunciation, sacrifice, loyalty, charm, prayer, and above all heroic actions by which the poet merits his lady in a manner comparable to attaining the compassion of Our Lady. This courtly "liturgy" could thus direct its energy not only to the lady but to the pilgrimage and quest for the "holy" grail. These developments may reflect the ongoing efforts of the medieval world to come to grips with its twin heritage of classical and Christian literature, with the mother-goddess cults of antiquity – both Celtic and Greco-Roman – and the early church designation of Mary as "God-bearer," with eros and agape.

The romances of the troubadours thus interweave religious and secular love. The knight-hero's yearning for his unattainable lady parallels the monastic-mystic's love from afar and yearning for union with God; and the challenges and obstacles to be overcome in the knightly quest for the Grail are parallels to the "knightly" combats of the mystic striving for God. All are "tests of love." The knight's hope for the grace mysteriously given by his distant lady parallels the mystic's prayer for the grace of the Virgin Mary.

Distinguishing, let alone unraveling, the warp and woof of the medieval tapestry of love is beyond the compass – not to mention the author's skill – of this little book. There is some comfort to be had in Jaeger's statement: "Courtly literature was never anything other than a literature of questioned presuppositions. It has not been possible to define a 'system' of courtly love, or reduce it to a definition or series of definitions." And, "Courtly love is not a doctrine, but a large grid crisscrossed with conflicting opinions." We shall leave aside that other medieval literary expression of love, the fabliaux. These tales tended to be crude parodies of sexuality that ridiculed husbands and demeaned women, regaling audiences with descriptions of genitalia and the deflowering of virgins, as well as serving as cautionary tales. Another expression of pre-troubadour poetry was called Goliard, the appellation of which is unclear but perhaps relates to the Latin *Golias* for the giant Goliath, the adversary of righteousness. These wandering poets, probably unemployed students and clerics, celebrated the attractions of wenching, drinking, and gambling. An example from the *Carmina Burana* is the song, "Under the Linden Tree" relating the oft-told tale of the young virgin beset by a wandering knight, shepherd, or – in this case – a vagabond. A couple of the verses give the sense of a bawdy tale.

> One day I went off the fields
> *to pluck me a bouquet:*
> but a vagabond lay there, with plans
> *to pluck ME, so to say!*

Unlike Goliard verse, the courtly romance was a new kind of literature whose authors first compiled and worked with classical and Celtic materials and manifested a dominant interest in the subjective realm of feeling, especially for love, and strove to reconcile such ennobling love with the received tradition – both classical and Christian – that suspected sexuality. The term "courtly love" – *amour courtois* – came into usage in the late nineteenth century in an article by Gaston Paris on Chrétien de Troyes' "Le Chevalier de la Charrete" ("The Knight of the Cart" or "Lancelot"). Paris's delineation of the term – the illegitimate character of love between Lancelot and King Arthur's wife, Guinevere; Lancelot's inferior position to Guinevere; the ennobling force of such love; and that such love was governed by a code of conduct as were courtesy and chivalry – gained acceptance as a universal definition of courtly love. More recent studies have recognized that this concept of love with its new valorization of the woman, arising in the twelfth century, not only varies by genre, region, and time but also may be too narrow a definition of a broad literature that strove to reconcile virtue and sex. The vocabulary likewise varies from the *fin amour* (refined or noble love; Chaucer spoke of "gentil loving;" in today's terms, "perfect," "true" or "romantic" love) of the troubadours of southern France to the *Minne* (*amor*) of German poets. Troubadours were poets and poet-musicians of France who in the south wrote in *langue d'oc*, the language of Provençal, and in the north of France their counterparts, *trouvères*, wrote in a language closer to modern French, *langue d'oil*. These poet-musicians belonged to the literate class of clerics and court figures adept in Latin and whose work helped to inspire the development of vernacular poetry. Around 1292, Dante noted that not more than 150 years earlier there arose the first poets who expressed themselves in the languages of southern France and Italy. They began to compose in the vernacular, Dante said, to make their verse understandable to women for whom Latin verse would have been too difficult to understand.

The best known popular collection of these songs is a selection of some 20 poems from the *Carmina Burana* for chorus and orchestra by Carl Orff. The *Carmina Burana* ("Songs of Beueren") is named after the Benedictine monastery in Bavaria where the manuscript was found. Most of the songs go back to the twelfth century during the reigns of Louis VII and Philippe Auguste of France, Friedrich Barbarossa of Germany, and Henry II of England and his wife Eleanor of Aquitaine (1122–1204), the granddaughter of William IX (1071–1127)

Duke of Aquitaine, the first of the troubadours. Eleanor's patronage of troubadour literature was continued by her daughter Marie, Countess of Champagne.

The collected songs of the *Carmina Burana* include satires and odes to drinking, gaming, religion, morality, and love. An example of the latter from Parlett's translation is "Love Rules Everything."

> Love rules everything – controls
> all the movement of our souls
> to its preappointed goals:
> vies with honey-sweetness, yes –
> and with gall in bitterness.
> . . .
> Cupid hovers in the air
> loosing darts off everywhere:
> every belle desires to pair
> with a beau to suit herself –
> none must be left on the shelf: . . .

Another example extols Cupid and Venus, the Latin names for our old friends Eros and Aphrodite.

> we're all after Cupid's prize:
> we who win it
> find within it
> sights reserved for lovers' eyes.
> Venus orders – let's obey:
> loudly voicing
> and rejoicing,
> we shall have her every day!

The courtly romance par excellence is Tristan and Isolde, the forerunner of Arthurian sagas, and the Lancelot and Guinevere romance. This "tale of love and death" has been translated into all the European languages and its popularity lives on in Richard Wagner's opera, modern novels, and movies. De Rougemont states of the legend: "Happy love has no history. Romance only comes into existence where love is fatal, frowned upon and doomed by life itself. What stirs lyrical poets to their finest flights is neither the delight of the senses nor the fruitful contentment of the settled couple; not the satisfaction of love, but its *passion*. And passion means suffering." Such passion may be understood as the height of eros because the rapture is precisely *not* in the capture but in the quest. Indeed, the more obstacles encountered, the more passionate the love. The quest fulfilled is no longer a quest. The elusiveness, the distance (love from afar) of the woman was indispensable to the development and maintenance of desire and passion. The woman, once attained, is no longer striven for. That is also why courtly love celebrated love from afar, that is, unattainable love of a woman of a higher social class, a woman married to the lord or king. It appears to be love in love with love, rather than a person. According to Jaeger: "The charm of a love hedged in by all sorts of restrictions on the physical is a peculiar mystery of the western erotic tradition. To renounce what appears essential to love gives love special allure." To be sure, courtly love also celebrated adultery; but that may be because medieval culture did not view marriage as a consummation of love but rather a social, economic, and – for upper classes – political arrangement. Indeed, as already noted, even within marriage sexual relations for pleasure rather than procreation was viewed as adulterous. One theory of courtly love is that if love was to be had, it had to be outside of marriage. Medieval culture did not share the claim of the pop tune of the 1950s oft-rendered by Doris Day that love and marriage go together like a horse and carriage.

The love that is imposed upon Tristan and Isolde is that passionate love that became a theme of European literature.

It is the consummate passion before which everything else fades: the courtly world and even Tristan's wife, Isolde of the White Hands, whom he has not once touched because of his passion for *the* Isolde, the Isolde married to his uncle, King Mark. There are many variations of the story, but the main threads may be briefly summarized. Tristan is entrusted to bring Isolde safely from her kingdom to that of his uncle King Mark with whom she is to wed. Isolde's mother had prepared a love potion so that her daughter and the king will have a marriage of love. However – by accident? – Isolde offers the potion to Tristan during their journey. There is, de Rougemont states, a religious aspect to the story. "The irrevocable drinking of the potion, which appears at the time to be due to chance, but which looks afterwards as if everything had conspired to bring it about, symbolizes a soul's *election* by omnipotent Love, its being unexpectedly seized by its vocation as if in its own despite." Jaeger states: "They drank eternal love and their death at the same time, and the story serves up this brew vicariously and eucharistically to the noble hearts of the audience, . . . Their tragic love 'gives us life' because it is 'bread' to all noble hearts." It is the allegory of the insuperable and the irrational, the two lovers are linked to one another and they are robbed of consciousness of all other commitments. The lovers have lost the world and the world them.

The Arthurian romances found their major exponent in Chrétien de Troyes (c.1135–c.1183), a contemporary and compatriot of Andreas Capellanus, author of *De Arte Honeste Amandi* (*The Art of Courtly Love*, c.1180). Almost nothing is known of these two poets apart from their works; even their names tell us only that the former was a Christian of Troyes and the latter, Andrew, was a chaplain. Both however were associated with the literary circle associated with the court of Troyes and its influential Countess Marie, daughter of

Eleanor of Aquitaine. The number of surviving manuscripts and translations of their works up to the sixteenth century indicate their great popularity. Chrétien developed such characters as Lancelot and introduced the theme of the search for the Holy Grail. He explored the ways of love in his literary works: adulterous love in *Lancelot*, married love in *Erec et Enide* and *Yvain*, and quasi-sacred love in *Perceval ou le Conte du Graal*. Chrétien, like his contemporary Capellanus, expresses ambivalent – even contradictory – views of courtly love. Although he wrote of adulterous love, he also opposed the destructive and socially alienating passions of a knightly society. In *Erec and Enide*, Erec, an Arthurian knight, fell in love with the truly poor Enide (of course she is the most beautiful maiden in the entire world!) and marries her. However, to the dismay of the court, the young hero now cared about nothing else than Enide and abandoned his service in arms and knighthood. "Erec loved her with such a tender love that he cared no more for arms, nor did he go to tournaments, nor have any desire to joust; but he spent his time in cherishing his wife." The pacifist slogan "make love not war" was even less popular then than during the Vietnam War. With Erec's manhood in question, Enide lets slip talk she hears from the court that laments Erec's love-sick turn from chivalry. Dubious about Enide's loyalty and love, and eager to prove he's no lapdog, Erec sets out on a series of knightly adventures with only Enide in tow. After a series of incredibly violent encounters with evil knights and giants and a near death experience, Erec proves he is even more the knight than before, and he sees the proof of Enide's love when apparently dead he sees her reject marriage with another knight. Together with her – knighthood is not recaptured without love – he overcomes a series of obstacles, which restores him to the society of knights to the joy of the court. The story ends with wonderful allegorical last adventure I leave for your own discovery. The major point however is that in contradiction to theories of courtly love, Enide had (unwittingly?) set up Erec whose ego then impelled him to seek and overcome obstacles, and she remains Erec's friend, lover, and spouse. Only in an apparent rejection is he able to recognize her perfect love. Because Enide held to her husband through all the contests, she proved the permanence of her feelings. Although Chrétien describes their love several times as bodily union ("together their hearts united in bed and they kissed"), their feelings for one another, and to the poet this is essentially more important, are the foundation of a socially usable relationship: Eric is allowed to become the ideal knight, Enide the ideal lady. Their love story contradicts both the claim that only unhappy love has a history (Tristan and Isolde) and that "happy families are all alike" (the modern romance by Tolstoy, *Anna Karenina*).

While Chrétien also wrote of adultery, it seems according to his work *Cligés* that he was not – if you will – personally enamored by the theme and left that poem incomplete. Andrew the Chaplain had no comparable compunction. Indeed, he claims clergy make the best lovers due to their "experienced knowledge" and boasts of his own "art of soliciting nuns" but with the cautionary note that the "solaces" of nuns bring the danger of civil punishment and divine wrath. Capellanus begins *The Art of Courtly Love* with his famous definition: "Love is a certain inborn suffering derived from the sight of and excessive meditation upon the beauty of the opposite sex, which causes each one to wish above all things the embraces of the other and by common desire to carry out all of love's precepts in the other's embrace."

The Art of Courtly Love, ostensibly written because his friend Walter wanted to learn the art of love, has three parts. The first two – in length over 85 percent of the book! – describe love and how to acquire it, the third part rejects the first two. The bulk of the book describes by means of injunctions, dialogues, and debates held at "courts of love" how to become the disciple of Cupid and Venus, that is, basically how to gain and live "by sex alone." "[W]hatever lovers do has as its only object the obtaining of the solaces of the lower part [of the body], for there is fulfilled the whole effect of love, at which all lovers aim and without which they think they have nothing more than certain preludes to love." Love is enhanced by its secrecy and obstacles such as jealousy; both of which are intrinsic to love since by his definition it is adultery. "[A] precept of love tells us that no woman, even if she is married, can be crowned with the reward of the King of Love unless she is seen to be enlisted in the service of Love himself outside the bonds of wedlock." That is why "everybody knows that love can have no place between husband and wife." Among the reasons why love is not possible within marriage is that "the too ardent lover, as we are taught by the apostolic law, is considered an adulterer with his own wife." Capellanus argues that since "the punishment is always greater when the use of a holy thing [i.e., marriage] is perverted by misuse [ardent love] than if we practice the ordinary abuses" we should love outside marriage. Another reason echoes the views of Heloise's objection to marriage to Abelard: only outside marriage is love free; once married, love is a duty.

The first two parts end with "The Rules of Love" "which the King of Love is said to have proclaimed with his own mouth and to have given in writing to all lovers." The first of these 31 rules reads: "Marriage is no real excuse for not loving." The "rules" reflect the troubadours' views of courtly love. Every lover is to keep the rules faithfully "under threat of punishment by the King of Love. These laws the whole court received in their entirety and promised forever to obey in order to avoid punishment by Love."

The third part of his book, "The Rejection of Love," renounces all that went before. "[N]o man, so long as he devotes himself to the service of love, can please God by any other works, even if they are good ones. For God hates, and in both testaments commands the punishment of, those whom he sees engaged in the works of Venus outside the bonds of wedlock or caught in the toils of any sort of passion." The "foul and shameful acts of Venus" put man "lower than a beast" and hand him "over to the flames of ever-burning Gehenna!" A strange contradiction that has puzzled readers since the book was written. Satire? Irony? On the one hand, Capellanus's retraction seems hardly more than a pro forma imitation of Ovid's scheme and a chance to ring all the changes on the misogyny of church tradition. On the other hand, he ends with acknowledging that he seems "to present two different points of view." That is because he "tried to assent" to Walter's "simple and youthful request" to know about love. But learning how to sin does not mean one ought to! "If you wish to practice the system, you will obtain . . . all the delights of the flesh in fullest measure; but the grace of God, the companionship of the good, and the friendship of praiseworthy men you will with good reason be deprived of, and you will do great harm to your good name, and it will be difficult for you to obtain the honors of the world."

These romances of courtly love with their rules for the "games people play," and their ludic character remained popular for centuries, indeed they continue to inform contemporary romances. Their use of allegory, paralleling the dominant allegorical exegesis of medieval biblical interpretation, continued in the thirteenth century in the famous and exceedingly popular *Romance of the Rose* authored by Guillaume de Lorris and Jean de Meun. Their celebrations of erotic passion were also contemporary social satires, often misogynistic, and – especially in the *Romance of the Rose* – critiques of the church and the Mendicant Orders. In response, by the end of the Middle Ages, reactions came from theologians such as Jean Gerson, chancellor of the University of Paris, and the woman poet, Christine de Pizan. Her *Epistle to the God of Love* (1399) warned women of the snares set by the game of courtly love. Courtly love is seen by her as the abuse of women for the satisfaction of men. She also contrasted the tenderness and mercy of women to the cruelty of men.

Scholars have debated whether there ever was such a social phenomenon as "courtly love" or whether it was largely the literary fiction of the poets. In a feudal culture which prized honor, skill at arms, and legitimate descent, adultery – especially with the lord's wife – would have been a dangerous game, not to mention a game condemned by the church.

What is striking about of the prevalence of courtly love stories and especially the works of Chrétien and Andreaus is that they burst on the stage between the tragic affair of Abelard and Heloise and the extended drama of the church's tightening grip on medieval Europe. Were the troubadours and their literature but a ludic intermission; court jesters more than court lovers; a call to "lighten up" in the so-called "Dark Ages"? The passion, the suffering, of Heloise and Abelard was not that of Tristan and Isolde. The real lovers were not in love with love but with each other. Abelard and Heloise did not portray their love as service to the love god (Eros); they were not on a quest for transcendence or a transcendent spirituality, but were enjoying the ordinary – the human mutuality and reciprocity of sexual relations. They chose each other and were not predestined by Eros's love potion. Abelard and Heloise did not need a manual such as *The Art of Love*, but only each other.

On the other side of the courtly love came the church's project to complete the "Christianization" of Europe. The so-called age of faith was marked by the rise of the new mendicant orders of Francis (1181/2–1226) and Dominic (1170–1221), the hegemony of theology in the universities with Thomas Aquinas (c.1225–1274) providing the theological architecture for medieval and modern Catholicism, the rule of clerical celibacy becoming the law of the church (Second Lateran Council, 1139), and the establishment powers – "the most Christian king" of France, St. Louis (1214–1270) and the ruler of the papacy, Innocent III (1160–1216). While in the early days of the church Tertullian asked what Athens had to do with Jerusalem, i.e., philosophy with revealed religion, no one seemed in these latter days of ecclesiastical and national consolidations to be asking what Cupid and Venus had to do with Jesus. How did the God of Love of the troubadours relate to the "God is love" of the New Testament? It is clear that the literary and plastic arts and also theology shared the same language so that the interweaving of sacred and profane is not surprising. It has been argued that the new language of love developed in the twelfth century not only because of the increased "Latinity" with recovery of Ovid among other classical writers, but also because of the new spirituality of the Cistercian monks. Bernard of Clairvaux was not alone among them in his fascination with the Song of Songs and expressing the relationship to God in the intimate and erotic terms used for that of a lover and beloved. It is interesting that the church did not condemn courtly love, at least not in any formal sense. How could it when its own saints latched on to it with their bridal mysticism? Or, could it be that courtly love was never perceived as a threat, but only a diversion for a waning warrior culture?

Courtly love, of course, did not die or even fade away. It lived on in satire and comedy such as Boccaccio's *Decameron* and Cervantes' *Don Quixote* and then into today's soap operas and musicals such as *The Man from La Mancha*. Shakespeare's

Romeo and Juliet live on not only in English classes but on stage in *West Side Story*. And the mystics' expressions of Christian love also continue to inform modern piety. As one of those monastic pioneers, Richard of St. Victor (d. 1173) wrote: "There are many degrees of love and great are the differences between them. Who is able really to differentiate them – or even to enumerate them?"

Chapter 7

Faith Formed by Love: Scholasticism

The twelfth-century "Ovidian age" with its (re)discovery of human love with all its individualized and personalized passions – the deathly passion of Tristan and Isolde; the spiritual passion of the mystics; female mystical passion for intimacy with Jesus; Bernardine passion for Christ's embrace and kiss – would indeed be a hard act to follow. What happens to these rivalries, mixtures, and syntheses of eros and agape with the advent of the great scholastic systems of the High Middle Ages? What happens to warmth and passion when it is "ordered" in a theological system?

The theological system of the High Middle Ages most often held up as the epitome of scholastic genius is that of the Dominican Thomas Aquinas (c.1225–1274). What he has to tell us about love is significant not only because of his stature as a medieval theologian but also because of the continuing importance of his works for Roman Catholic theology. Canonized in 1323 and declared a Doctor of the Church (i.e., official teacher) in 1567, the works of the "Angelic Doctor" were made mandatory for all Roman Catholic students of theology in 1879 by Pope Leo XIII, and his teaching authority was reiterated in 1923 by Pope Pius XI.

Thomas's fame as the theologians' theologian rests upon his incorporation of the greatest intellectual challenge of his time – Aristotle's philosophy – into an exposition of Christian faith that in structure has been compared to the achievement of the gothic cathedrals of his day. Thomas left an immense body of work including, but not limited to, commentaries on the works of predecessors such as Peter Lombard, Boethius, and Dionysius the Pseudo-Areopagite; commentaries on philosophers, especially Aristotle; numerous exegetical commentaries on biblical books; various writings on disputed questions; and the two works for which he is best known, the *Summa contra Gentiles* (a text for missionaries) and the *Summa Theologica* ("Summary of Theology").

Thomas discusses *caritas*, charity, in both his *Summa Theologiae* and his treatise *De Caritate* (*On Charity*). The latter is one of a series of 11 treatises on various subjects compiled from his *Quaestiones Disputatae*, collections of disputed questions that were academic exercises which included arguments pro and con. Kendzierski's "Introduction" to her translation of *De Caritate* notes the similarity in style and content between the *Summa*'s discussion of love and the treatise on love. The main difference between the two writings is their respective purposes. "Whereas the *Disputed Questions* were intended for the proficient, the *Summa*, as St. Thomas states in the Prologue, ought not only to instruct the proficient, but should instruct beginners." Anyone who picks up the *Summa* for the first time may well surmise that "beginners" in the Middle Ages were exceptionally learned. Kerr suggests that the *Summa Theologica* was designed for the instructors of beginners: "The *Summa* reads more like the second-level reflective course which might follow years of studying the biblical and patristic texts, and of hearing doctrinal issues disputed in the schools."

The flavor of *On Charity*, as well as its difference in style from our prior "A, B, C's" of love – Abelard and Heloise, Bernard of Clairvaux, Courtly Love poets – may be seen from its list of questions:

> The first point of inquiry is whether charity is something created in the soul, or is it the Holy Spirit Itself? 2. Whether charity is a virtue? 3. Whether charity is the form of the virtues? 4. Whether charity is one virtue? 5. Whether charity is a special virtue? 6. Whether there can be charity with mortal sin? 7. Whether the object to be loved out of charity is a rational nature? 8. Whether loving one's enemies comes from the perfection of a counsel? 9. Whether there is some order in charity? 10. Whether charity can be perfect in this life? 11. Whether all are bound to perfect charity? 12. Whether charity, once possessed, can be lost? 13. Whether charity can be lost through one act of mortal sin?"

It appears that the personal "A, B, C's" of love mentioned above are succeeded by an intellectual tour de force. Indeed, according to Brady: "Unlike Augustine or even Bernard, a detailed knowledge of Thomas's life is not necessary to understand his work." One biographical incident, however, suggests that early on Thomas banished eros from his personal life. His teenage decision to enter the fairly recently founded Order of Preachers, the Dominicans, upset his noble family's more prestigious plans for him. Efforts to dissuade him, including imprisoning him in the family castle, came to naught. As a last resort they tried to tempt him by putting a courtesan in his room. In response, Thomas snatched a burning brand from the fireplace and chased the woman from his room, barring her reentry by burning a huge black cross into the door.

Obviously such a story has far more entertainment than explanatory value. Yet it may be argued that there is a certain displacement of eros in the sense of human desire and love from human relationships into a theological system of virtue capped by *caritas*, "charity." The presuppositions for this development are both theological and philosophical. The Augustinian schema of "ordered" love, *caritas*, vs. "disordered" love, *cupiditas*, provided a tradition that posited an ascent to God enabled by God's love to humankind. The philosophical logic of Aristotle that like is known only by like, encouraged medieval theologians to posit that if there is to be fellowship with God it requires elevation to God's level; sinful human-kind is unlike God and therefore needs to be purified by God's love in order to rise to God. Wadell provides a brief summary: Thomas, like Augustine, poses the subject of love in terms of the "pursuit of happiness," "an odyssey toward happiness with God." "To be happy is to be in love with the best possible good, and for Thomas that is God. A happy person is one who lives in love with God. Lovers of God are happy because love brings likeness, and loving God makes us enough like God to find joy in God."

Here again we can see the appropriation also of the Augustinian synthesis of eros and agape. The biblical sense of the motivational force of God's love, agape, has now however become increasingly a teleological force, that is eros. In his extensive chapter, "Aquinas on Eros," Vacek remarks that Thomas's appropriation of the Hellenistic eros teleology – "Every nature *desires* its own being and *its own perfection*" (Aquinas) – borders on "psychological egoism" and "ethical egoism." "Aquinas sometimes sounds like an eudaimonistic utilitarian: 'Of necessity, every man desires happiness. . . . Happy is the man that has all he desires.' . . . Aquinas asks how we can attain happiness. Though Aquinas did not in fact do so, much Catholic ethics under the inspiration of this question tended to make morality a science of human happiness and of the various means to achieve our final happiness. Religiously, Aquinas courts this *anthropocentrism* [author's emphasis] by proposing two correlative premises: 'Happiness means the acquisition of the last end' and God is that which completely satisfies the human appetite.''

In directional terms, the love of God flowing ''down'' to the creation, to humankind, in service to the neighbor, now facilitates an ''upward'' effort to acquire salvation. As mentioned earlier, this is most graphically seen in the widespread medieval images of ascent to heaven, especially that of the ladder of virtues that reaches from earth to heaven. The ladder imagery that pictures the Christian's ascent to heaven was a very popular depiction of the scholastic theology of ordered love. The image portrays the synthesis of Hellenistic eros and Christian agape for the very desire and drive to self-fulfillment (eros) is made possible by God's enablement (agape). The ''Ladder of Virtues'' in the late twelfth-century manuscript *Hortus Deliciarum* (''Garden of Delights''), the rungs of which correspond to the virtues to be acquired for salvation, is shown with climbers representing the medieval social hierarchy at different levels on the ladder, the highest figure being an allegorical representation of Caritas, who receives the crown of life from the hand of God extending from the cloud-shrouded top of the ladder. All the other figures are literally bent down toward what attracts them, and hence falling off the ladder. They thereby depict *cupiditas*, the disordered love Augustine defined as sin, that is, the love for inferior or earthly delights. The lowest figures are a knight and his wife who are attracted to worldly things of the flesh. Next is a cleric bent toward his food-laden table and lady-friend; and to his left a priest is tempted by money. Above them, a monk is falling from the weight of money in the sack around his neck; and above him a recluse is tipping toward a soft bed, and a hermit toward his small garden. The object of temptation is inversely proportional to the level of virtue attained. The monk, recluse, and hermit are far from the material temptations of the world, but the apparently more simple objects of temptation have taken their place. Thus it is not the objects themselves which cause the climbers to fall but rather that the climbers' thoughts and desires turn toward them. Caritas, at the top of the ladder, is the virtue that each of these figures is called to attain.

The pervasive medieval iconography of the ladder to heaven presents *caritas*, love, as the highest virtue. Indeed, of the theological virtues – faith, hope, and love – love is supreme, the highest rung below which is hope and then faith. In scholastic theological terms, faith is formed by love (*fides caritate formata*). The ladder image conveys Thomas Aquinas's expressions: "love is called the aim of all virtues;" "love is called the mother of all virtues;" "love is the mover or rouser of all virtues;" and "love is the root of all virtues."

Caritas, however, is no longer a natural ability for humankind since the original fall into sin. To be sure, humankind has the natural capabilities of virtue – the natural or cardinal virtues celebrated since Plato – prudence, justice, fortitude, and temperance. The wise person realizes that his or her drive for happiness depends upon the cultivation and practice of these virtues. The question for Thomas is how the ultimate goal of humankind, the enjoyment of God, may be attained. Since in terms of Aristotelian logic like is known by like, for humankind to know God necessitates becoming "like" God, that is, fulfilling God's law of love. How is that possible after the fall? The answer is that God in love for humankind infuses into persons by means of the church's sacraments the supernatural virtues of faith, hope, and love. Grace, God's love, thus does not destroy nature but completes it; there is continuity between the natural and supernatural, the right order of which is to move up the ladder from the natural to the supernatural, from the love of creation to the love of the Creator.

Miles provides a succinct overview of the ascent motif in her volume *The Image and Practice of Holiness*. After discussing the historical context of the ladder image in monastic spirituality she notes some of its inherent problems. First of all, even in the Middle Ages, it was not easily transferable from its monastic ascetic setting to a lay context of life in the world. The corollary to this is that the motif of ascent emphasized the privileged position – both socially and religiously – of the clerical life over that of the laity. We may add that that reinforces the sense that celibacy is on a higher religious plane than marriage. It also implicitly if not explicitly denigrates the world: "attention to the world of the senses is presented as a distraction from, rather than a clue to, its creator." She cites a passage from the famous Renaissance humanist, Erasmus (1469–1536) that illustrates both the influence of the ascent motif and the continuing pervasiveness of Platonism: "Transfer your love to something permanent, something celestial, something incorruptible, and you will love more coolly this transitory and fleeting form of the body."

The social implications of scholasticism's ordered love, from the lower to the higher, nature to supernature, creation to Creator, may be seen in the medieval church's broad sense of love to the neighbor manifest in its suspicion of sexuality, emphasis upon mandatory clerical celibacy, and relations to the poor. The conflicted and conflicting views of sexuality in Western culture – continuing into our own time! – have multiple roots, some of which we have already suggested. The labeling of sexual relations not directly intended for procreation as mortal sin did not of course do a lot for the cultivation of passionate marriages. Ironically, the effort to privilege celibacy and to dampen the erotic within marriage created extra-marital outlets not only in courtly love and mysticism but also in publicly condoned prostitution.

But what sense can be made of the co-existence in medieval society of a clerically imposed sexual stringency and publicly condoned prostitution? Among the factors influencing this development were the church's view of marriage, and the rise of cities and urban commerce. The church's views of marriage, as already indicated, had roots in the association of the doctrine of original sin with a sexual origin. Augustine was not the first, but certainly one of the most influential Western theologians, to posit that since sin originates with Adam, it must be hereditary. The logical development of Augustinian doctrine that sexualized sin continued into scholasticism.

Theological reflections about marriage also continued basic Augustinian doctrine, albeit with some differences, positing that marriage, established in Paradise before sin, was for the propagation of humankind. After the Fall, the hitherto unknown libido became the driving force of sexuality and thus marriage becomes the remedy against this libido. Sexual intercourse due to lust is condemnable, but becomes pardonable by the goods or values of marriage. These goods include the spiritual union and companionship of the spouses and the procreation of children. The doctrine of marriage as a sacrament developed gradually in the eleventh to the twelfth centuries, partly as a response to heretical views which viewed marriage as an intrinsic evil. Although marriage in the medieval period was basically a social and economic relationship, that did not preclude an affective aspect in the choice of spouse. In his article on marriage, Francis Schüssler Fiorenza notes that French theologians in particular advocated that marriage requires consent, and that in turn "led to an emphasis on love within marriage." He refers to Richard of St. Victor's (d. 1173) *Of the Four Degrees of Passionate Love* which gives priority to conjugal love among human affections.

While Thomas Aquinas stressed friendship in marriage, his indebtedness to Aristotelian philosophy ("the female is a misbegotten male") reinforced a crass view that women are biologically inferior to men, hardly a view conducive to reciprocal and mutual love relationships. In his *Summa Theologica* where he treats the creation of woman he argues that woman is subject to man because she is "defective and misbegotten" and because reason predominates in man. "For good order would have been wanting in the human family if some were not governed by others wiser than themselves. So by such a kind of subjection woman is naturally subject to man, because in man the discretion of reason predominates."

The historical context may provide some clues to the apparent conflicts between the church's theological and doctrinal positions and the social endorsement and support of forms of "free love." Romantic notions of the Middle Ages gloss over the all-too-frequent brutalities of the age. In the context of "noble" society, the development of courtly love was not merely entertainment but an effort to curb knightly violence, to instill *courtoisie*, rules of courtesy and manners. The High Medieval development of cities and commerce with their anonymity and impersonal money transactions created its own forms of conflict, poverty, and social unrest. In his study, *Medieval Prostitution*, Rossiaud highlights especially the prevalence of sexual violence, largely taking the form of gang rapes involving extreme brutality. Then – as all too often today – rape was considered a minor crime the cause of which was attributed to the victim. After all, the theologically and philosophically endorsed views of the time had long asserted male superiority and female lust.

Rossiaud argues that the mayhem and violence of the medieval towns is related to the prevalence of adolescent gangs out to prove their masculinity and challenge the social order. "City notables and heads of large households had a stake in quelling this turbulence. They offered their sons, their domestics and their working-men liberal opportunities for municipally-sponsored fornication (and they took advantage of it themselves)." The argument here is that the establishment of municipal brothels and their civic regulation was an effort to establish social control and preserve marital stability by protecting the virtue of wives and daughters from rowdy youths and lusty clerics. Prostitutes were understood to have a function – indeed, municipal authorities and others termed it a *ministerium,* a ministry – that "contributed to the defense of collective order." Their work protected women "of estate" from unruliness, and they tempered the aggression of the young and outsiders.

Rossiaud reviews the variety of intellectual acrobatics by which theologians and preachers accommodated the social reality by refining categories of sin and placing common fornication low on the list. In his *Summa* Thomas writes that God allows various evils to exist because without them greater goods might disappear or greater evils appear. The rationale par excellence, however, was a pseudo-Augustinian gloss that appeared in the thirteenth century: "The public woman is in society what bilge is in [a ship at sea] and the sewer pit in a palace. Remove this sewer and the entire palace will be contaminated."

The church accommodated these attitudes toward nature and its forces (the municipal brothel is "Nature's workshop"). Fornication with a married person remained a mortal sin, but fornication with a prostitute did not threaten to disrupt the social order of marriage and urban life and thus was at most a venial sin. Such tolerance reflected also the view that since the prostitute was not only unattached but selling her body – a merchant in her own way – lust was not involved. Likewise, priestly fornication in brothels could be the subject of jokes but not condemnation by the populace. Priestly concubinage on the other hand was condemned by the church for it was not only sin, it also threatened to deplete the wealth of the church if clerics thought they could pass church property on to their sons. At the same time, these currents stimulated the theologians toward revised views of marriage that included an emphasis upon mutual consent by the future spouses and an acknowledgment that pleasure in sexual relationships was a value in marriage.

Love of neighbor was also manifest in the rethinking of the biblical mandate to care for the poor. Now that urban mer-
ꞌchants and commerce were beginning to edge out a society of knights and monasteries, avarice and charity displaced pride and humility as the main vice and virtue. Earlier monasticism with its focus on humility had selected Matthew's version of the "Sermon on the Mount" that read: "Blessed are the poor in spirit, for theirs is the kingdom of heaven." The monks of the Benedictine monasteries – including reformers such as Bernard of Clairvaux – came from proud noble families and hence understood the sin to be combated was pride. The new monastic movements of the High Middle Ages – the Order of Preachers (Dominicans) and the Franciscans – arose in the new milieu of urban and commercial development that spawned actual poverty on a new scale. The sin they saw around them was not so much pride as avarice; hence they focused on the parallel biblical text in Luke: "Blessed are you who are poor, for yours is the kingdom of heaven." The increase of urban poverty and economic vulnerability stimulated the view that the proper index of religious devotion was the love of the neighbor that not only prayed for the soul but also distributed sustenance for the body. The Dominican and Franciscan Orders adopted a policy of corporate as well as individual poverty, and focused their ministry on the issues of urban wealth and poverty. Now, instead of being cloistered away in walled monasteries, the new monastic movements roamed the cities and preached in the vernacular as intermediaries between the wealthy and the poor. The man who epitomized the new awareness of the neighbor in the poor was Francis of Assisi (1182–1226).

Unlike Thomas Aquinas, whose theological contribution stands on its own without knowledge of his biography,

Francis's contribution is inseparable from his person. In the story of Francis there is a remarkable conjunction of medium and message; he not only proclaimed the reign of love, he lived it. Francis had a privileged youth thanks to his father, Pietro Bernadone, a wealthy cloth merchant. Little is known of Francis's childhood. He did receive an elementary education from the local priests of Assisi, but was far more enamored of the knightly life and troubadour praise of it. His visions of military glory seem not to have been significantly dimmed by a year's imprisonment in Perugia following the Perugian defeat of Assisi forces at the battle of Collestrada. Francis next enlisted in the campaign led by a dashing knight, Walter of Brienne, against imperial forces. Illness and religious dreams prompted Francis to return to Assisi where his increasing introspection and religious reflection led him in a startling new direction, albeit with a few bumps in the road. Encountering a poor leper – one of the most feared, repugnant, and marginalized persons of the time – Francis overcame his disgust, embraced the man (a putative means to his own social ostracism), and gave him all the money he had. Parental as well as social disapproval escalated as Francis took cloth from his father's shop, sold it and his horse, and threw the money away when the local priest did not accept it for repairing a chapel. Pietro denounced Francis as a thief and appealed to the bishop of Assisi for justice. In a public confrontation with his father, Francis stripped naked to give his clothes to his father, and exclaimed that Bernadone was no longer his father; his only father now was "Our Father" in heaven.

Such was Francis's dramatic but rather rocky start upon a life of absolute poverty. Like the troubadour lyrics which earlier appealed to him, he too now had his "lady." The difference is that she was not a love from afar, but became his spouse: "Lady Poverty." An early Franciscan treatise on holy poverty, *Sacrum Commercium* (*The Sacred Exchange between*

St. Francis and Lady Poverty), relates the "quest" for Lady
Poverty, "her whom his soul loved," undertaken by Francis.
The quest is, of course, an ascent "up to a great and high
mountain where God has placed her." Lady Poverty, aston-
ished by the rapid ascent of Francis and his companions, asks
why they came to her. "We wish to become servants of the
Lord of hosts,... We have heard that you are the queen of
virtues.... Casting ourselves at your feet, then, we humbly ask
you to agree to... be for us the way of arriving at the King of
glory, ..." They petition her in words echoing the Marian
antiphon: "Lady, we beg you through him and because of
him: 'despise not our petitions in our necessities, but deliver
us always from danger, [you who are] glorious and blessed
forever.'" About a century later, Dante immortalized in his
Divine Comedy Francis's pursuit of Lady Poverty who had been
made a widow by Christ's death on the cross:

> Bereft of her First Groom, she had had to stand
>   more than eleven centuries, scorned, obscure;
>   and, till he came, no man had asked her hand:...
> and none, at word of her fierce constancy,
>   so great, that even when Mary stayed below,
>   she climbed the Cross to share Christ's agony.
> But lest I seem obscure, speaking this way,
>   take Francis and Poverty to be those lovers.
>   That, in plain words, is what I meant to say.

Francis's quest for poverty was counter-cultural to the rising
new profit economy. He and his followers, known as mendicants for they supported themselves and their preaching
missions by begging, promoted charity by example and proclamation. In his article "Religion, The Profit Economy, and
St. Francis," Little wrote: "Charity held a special place in the
spirituality of the mendicant orders. The friars themselves
emulated the poverty of Jesus and the Apostles and thus

adopted the spiritual ideal of itinerancy and begging. They also emulated the evangelical models of caring for the sick, sharing with the needy, and keeping company with those shunted to the margins of society." An essential part of their preaching, Little continues, "reminded the relatively well-off of their continuing obligation to share their bounty with the poor."

Ironically, the counter-cultural move of the mendicant friars served to reinforce the profit economy of the time that openly violated the church's prohibition of usury. How did that happen? The preachers facilitated the wealthy to ascend the ladder of virtues toward the "gift of life," by exhorting charity to the poor. The mendicants, to cite Little again, "preached to . . . the rich. But they did not threaten the rich; instead they gave them comfort by justifying their ways of making money. The response of the wealthier class to the friars was explosive. They gave the friars shelter and sustenance when they arrived, and helped them build their churches and convents. They rushed to associate themselves with the friars in every way they could." What Francis and his followers contributed to the wealthy who desired heaven in spite of their usury was philanthropy; a means of giving alms through the intermediary of Francis.

The atoning power of philanthropy was not a new idea with Francis, but the tensions of the new economic context coupled with Francis's embodiment of a "respectable," that is, voluntary, poverty in contrast to the disreputable involuntary impoverishment of growing numbers of the late medieval urban populace revitalized the appeal of philanthropy. The apocryphal biblical writings of Tobit and Sirach had long provided warrants for the redemptive significance of charity. Charity was seen as a remedy for sin and – even better for a budding profit economy – an investment in heaven. Charity was a way of "laying up good treasure for yourself against the day of darkness; for all who practice it charity is an excellent

offering in the presence of the Most High'' (Tob. 4:9–11).
''For almsgiving delivers from death, and it will purge away
every sin'' (Tob. 12:9). Sirach, so esteemed by the Latin church
that by the third century it was known as Ecclesiasticus,
affirmed that almsgiving atones for sin as water extin-
guishes a blazing fire and that God hears the curses of the
poor (Ecclesiasticus 3:30; 4:1–6). The power of these verses
was enhanced by New Testament condemnations of the
wealthy and exhortations to give up everything and follow
Jesus (Matt. 19:24; Mark 10:25; Luke 18:25; Mark 10:17–21).
In this light it is no wonder that Francis and his mendicant
order were seen as a godsend. For example, Armstrong cites
''A Renewed Call to Penance'' that Francis addressed to ''all
mayors and consuls, magistrates and rulers throughout the
world'': ''Let us, therefore, have charity and humility and
give alms because it washes the stains of our sins from our
souls (cf. Tob. 4:11; 12:9). For though people lose everything
they leave behind in this world; they carry with them, however, the rewards of charity and the alms they have given for
which they will receive a reward and a fitting payment from
the Lord.''

Philanthropy justified the new profit economy; the wealthy
could have their cake and eat it too – they could make money
and gain salvation. This paradox, as Little calls it in his study
Religious Poverty and the Profit Economy in Medieval Europe, led
within a few decades of Francis's death to the Archbishop of
Pisa praising the merchants of his city and referring to Francis
as '' 'their merchant intermediary with God.' . . . St. Francis of
Assisi had become the patron and protector of merchants.''

Chapter 8

Faith Active in Love: Reformation

The understanding of love in the Reformation period shifted fundamentally from the Augustinian–medieval theological developments. For the Reformers, love is no longer conceived in terms of Plato's highest good or Aristotle's crown of virtue "baptized" as God's grant of "the crown of life," *caritas*, to those successfully ascending the ladder from vice to virtue. Already in one of the earliest Reformation writings, Luther's "Disputation Against Scholastic Theology" (1517), Aristotelian foundations for theology are decisively rejected: "An act of friendship is not...the most perfect means for obtaining the grace of God..." "Virtually the entire *Ethics* of Aristotle is the worst enemy of grace." "It is an error to say that no man can become a theologian without Aristotle." "Indeed, no one can become a theologian unless he becomes one without Aristotle." "Briefly, the whole of Aristotle is to theology as darkness is to light." "The grace of God...is not given so that good deeds might be induced more frequently and readily." The Augustinian synthesis of eros and agape, of an ordered love to God and neighbor, is rejected on the basis that no matter how much God's agape enables human eros to ascend the ladder of virtues the burden of proof for the ascent finally rests upon the person. The Reformation shifted the paradigm from God-assisted cooperation in salvation to the sole activity of God. A homely analogy contrasting monkeys and cats has been used to highlight this shift. When the mother monkey senses danger she calls her babies to climb up and cling to her back to be carried to safety. When the mother cat senses danger she grabs her kittens by the scruff of their necks and carries them to safety.

The love of God, then, from the perspective of the Reformation, is received through faith in God's promise of salvation, rather than achieved by the medieval triad of prayer, fasting, and alms. In contrast to the Aristotelian logic that since like can only know like fellowship with God must be on God's level, the Reformers proclaimed that fellowship with God occurs on the human level; God descends in love to humankind. The consequence of this "religionless" Christianity – that is, the freedom from striving toward heaven for salvation – was the release of resources and energy from an "otherworldly" ascent to gain the love of God to a this-worldly faith-rooted love to the neighbor. The "direction" of love did an about face from ascent to descent, from love to God to God's love flowing down to love of the neighbor. Social effects of this shift from "faith formed by love" to "faith active in love" included a revalorization of marriage and sexuality, and the institutionalization of love to the neighbor in the form of civic social welfare and universal education.

The shift in understanding love is evident in the conversion experience of Martin Luther (1483–1546). As a young monk, priest, and then professor of Bible at the University of Wittenberg, Luther reacted with despair to the biblical injunction to love God above all else and the neighbor as oneself. His sensitivity to the mixed motives of all lovers as well as his own, burdened his conscience and efforts to ascend in love to God. Luther experienced the striving to love God above all and the neighbor as himself tinged by either fear of punishment or hope of reward as basically love of self. Indeed, Luther came to define sin just that way, as being curved in upon the self, in contrast to Augustine's defining sin as being curved toward lesser goods. Such egoism, "a higher hedonism" if you will, is a vicious circle. What kind of God would put such a burden of proof for love upon sinners? Toward the end of his life, Luther recalled: "Though I lived as a monk without reproach, I felt that I was a sinner before God with an extremely disturbed conscience. . . . I hated the righteous God who punishes sinners." His conversion occurred when through study of the text of Romans 1:17 he came to realize that the love and righteousness of God is a gift not a demand. Luther expressed his sharp divergence from the medieval "order of love" in his discussion of God's promise to love humankind as a last will and testament sealed by the death of Christ. In *The Babylonian Captivity of the Church*, Luther wrote: "A testament, as everyone knows, is a promise made by one about to die, in which he designates his bequest and appoints his heirs. A testament, therefore, involves, first the death of the testator, and second, the promise of an inheritance and the naming of the heir." He then refers to the discussions of testament in Romans 4, Galatians 3–4, and Hebrews 9, concluding with the promise given at the Last Supper of Christ's body given "for you," "that is, for those who accept and believe the promise of the testator. For here it is faith that makes men heirs, . . ." Luther continued this theme of inheritance in his *Treatise on the New Testament, That Is, the Holy Mass*. Preparation for the sacrament "is all pure foolishness and self-deception, if you do not set before you the words of the testament. . . . You would have to spend a long time polishing your shoes, preening and primping to attain an inheritance if you had no letter and seal with which you could prove your right to it. But if you have a letter and seal, and believe, desire, and seek it, it must be given to you, even though you were scaly, scabby, stinking, and most filthy.'' In short, the sinner accepts that he or she is named as an heir in God's last will and testament, and since God has died, the will is in effect. In more prosaic language, again in *The Babylonian Captivity of the Church*: "First of all there is God's Word. After it follows faith; after faith, love; then love does every good work, . . . That is to say, that the author of salvation is not man, by any works of his own, but God through his promise; . . . " Such faith, Luther stated, "is followed by works as the body is followed by its shadow.''

In contrast to all pieties of achievement, then and now, Luther affirmed God's descent in Jesus to humankind rather than humankind's ascent to God. In opposition to the medieval renunciation of the world, epitomized by the image and metaphor of the ladder to heaven, Luther criticized any religion that prescribed "heavenward journeys" for such "travelers will break their necks.'' Thus in a sermon on the Gospel of John, Luther has Jesus say: "I have revealed to you in My Word what form I would assume and to whom you should give. You do not ascend into heaven, where I am seated at the right hand of My heavenly Father, to give Me something; no I come down to you in humility. I place flesh and blood before your door with the plea: "Give me a drink! . . . I do not need food in heaven. . . . I have had it announced to all the world that whatever is done to the least of My brethren is done to me.''

Luther did not write a specific tract on love, but he did set forth a thesis in his "Heidelberg Disputation'' (1518) that succinctly presents the distinction discussed earlier between eros and agape. Thesis 28 reads: "The love of God does not find, but creates, that which is pleasing to it. The love of

man comes into being through that which is pleasing to it.''
In explaining this thesis, Luther wrote:

> The first part is clear because the love of God which lives in man
> loves sinners, evil persons, fools, and weaklings in order to
> make them righteous, good, wise, and strong. Rather than
> seeking its own good, the love of God flows forth and bestows
> good. Therefore sinners are attractive because they are loved;
> they are not loved because they are attractive. For this reason
> the love of man avoids sinners and evil persons. Thus Christ
> says: ''For I came not to call the righteous, but sinners'' [Matt.
> 9:13]. This is the love of the cross, born of the cross, which turns
> in the direction where it does not find good which it may enjoy,
> but where it may confer good upon the bad and needy person.
> ''It is more blessed to give than to receive'' [Acts 20:35], says
> the Apostle.

Since for Luther salvation, we may say here the love of God,
is not the process or goal of life, but rather the presupposition
of life, his theology became a transvaluation of all values. Thus
his orientation to social issues was not in the mode of the
Aristotelian (and modern!) progress from vice to virtue. Love
to the neighbor is based upon neither self-realization nor upon
its results, but upon God's promise. Social ethics therefore does
not depend upon success, but upon God's promise: faith is
active in love.

Good works are not salvatory, but they do serve the neighbor. Since works are not ultimate but penultimate activities of
the sinner saved by the justifying God, they are this-worldly
rather than other-worldly, directed to the neighbor in response
to God's love. Thus Luther's social ethics are aptly described as
''the liturgy after the liturgy.'' In his ''Preface'' to the Leisnig
town *Ordinance of a Common Chest*, Luther wrote: ''Now there is
no greater service of God [*dienst Gottes* is equivalent to the
German word for worship, *Gottesdienst*] than Christian love

which helps and serves the needy, as Christ himself will judge and testify at the Last Day, Matthew 25[:31–46]." "The world would be full of worship if everyone served his neighbor, the farmhand in the stable, the boy in the school, maid and mistress in the home." By emphasizing that love to God occurred in the world, through the goods of the world – including one's beer vat, as he once said – Luther overcame the inherent religious separation of sacred and profane activity.

From the initial uproar over the "95 Theses" of 1517 to his death after mediating a dispute between the counts of Mansfeld in 1546, Luther remained center stage through the religious, economic, political, and social upheavals of the period. Throughout these upheavals and rapid social changes, people appealed to him for advice concerning every area of personal and social life. The multiplicity of social issues created as well as unleashed by Luther's initiation of reform may be approached under the rubric he used of the "three orders" or "estates" – the church, household (economy), and government (politics). According to Luther, these are the fundamental forms by which God's promise of creation constitutes human existence. In his *Confession Concerning Christ's Supper*, Luther related these forms to Christian love. "Above these three institutions and orders is the common order of Christian love, in which one serves not only the three orders, but also serves every needy person in general with all kinds of benevolent deeds, such as feeding the hungry, giving drink to the thirsty, forgiving enemies, praying for all men on earth, suffering all kinds of evil on earth, etc."

It is also important to recognize that the borders between the three estates are permeable, and the concerns of one estate frequently relate to the concerns of the other. Further, the estate of the household was broadly conceived to include not only marriage and the family, but also social welfare and local and national economic concerns.

Since, according to Luther, salvation is the source rather than the goal of life, Christians are called to celebrate the ordinary. Luther thus rejected every form of flight from the world with its suspicion of creation including the human body. Humankind is not called to flee the world but rather to engage the world for the common good. One early concrete demonstration of the new faith was clerical marriage. This was not just a matter of breaking church law; rather, the public rejection of mandatory clerical celibacy encompassed the new evangelical understanding of the relationship to God and the world.

Luther's confrontation with church authorities on this subject began with his *To the Christian Nobility of the German Nation Concerning the Reform of the Christian Estate*. Every priest should be free to marry because "before God and the Holy Scriptures marriage of the clergy is no offense." Clerical celibacy is not God's law but the pope's, and "Christ has set us free from all man-made laws, especially when they are opposed to God and the salvation of souls. . . . " Thus the pope has no more power to command celibacy than "he has to forbid eating, drinking, the natural movement of the bowels, or growing fat." Luther was well aware that the abolition of clerical celibacy would entail radical rethinking of church law, government, and property. Luther's application of evangelical theology to marriage and family de-sacramentalized marriage, making it a civil affair; de-sacralized the clergy making them tax-paying citizens, and re-sacralized the life of the laity for work in the world as signs of God's love; and joyfully affirmed God's good creation, including sexual relations.

As already noted, the medieval church viewed the celibate life as a meritorious work for salvation, and perpetuated patristic suspicions of sexuality as the font of original sin. Jerome's (c.342–420) view that virginity is the ideal state of Christian life ("Marriages fill the earth, virginity fills heaven") was repugnant and blasphemous to Luther. To Luther, sex is an aspect of God's good creation. Ozment, in *Protestants*, states that in contrast to the patristic and medieval tradition of asceticism, Luther and his colleagues "literally transferred the accolades Christian tradition heaped on the religious in monasteries and nunneries to marriage and the home.... 'Faith not virginity, fills paradise,' the Wittenberg pastor Johannes Bugenhagen retorted in the 1520s. 'Saint Jerome's unfortunate comment...must be corrected,' agreed the Lutheran poet Erasmus Alberus; 'let us rather say, "*Connubium replete coelum*, Marriage fills heaven.'"' Luther, in the words of Oberman, "excoriated repression of the sexual drive in the service of a higher perfection,...Luther wanted to liberate the Christian faith from this distortion: he could not accept the oppression of people down to their most intimate moments and warned of its devastating effects on society." In *Against the Spiritual Estate of the Pope and the Bishops Falsely So Called*, Luther asserted that men and women cannot do without one another because "to conceive children is as deeply implanted in nature as eating and drinking are. That is why God gave us and implanted into our body genitals, blood vessels, fluids, and everything else to accomplish it."

With marriage and the household estate came multiple responsibilities to the larger community and vice-versa. As Luther stated: "Marriage does not only consist of sleeping with a woman – anybody can do that – but of keeping house and bringing up children." Those who followed Luther saw in marriage not only a new joyous appreciation for sexual relations, but also a new respect for women as companions. Luther could not imagine life without women: "The home, cities, economic life and government would virtually disappear. Men cannot do without women. Even if it were possible for men to beget and bear children, they still couldn't do without women."

In 1525 Luther married Katherine von Bora who two years earlier had arrived in Wittenberg with other nuns who had escaped from a Cistercian convent. Their six children provided Luther with new insights into human and divine love. Stolt relates how Luther was surprised by the intensity of his love for his children, and thereby gained emotional insight into God the Father's love for humankind. He compared God's love and forgiveness of sin to his changing his children's diapers and the consequent removal of shit and stink. He often compared the stink of babies' diapers with the sins of adults – using the still prevalent phrase – "That stinks to high heaven!" Again, he drew the analogy between parents' love and care for their children to the merciful forgiving love of God.

Luther sought to redefine what his society thought appropriate for male and female behavior. As noted in the previous chapter, medieval society and theology sanctioned prostitution and civic brothels. The church tolerated prostitution because its gender values denigrated sex and also assumed that male desire was an anarchic, uncontrollable force that, if not provided an outlet, would pollute the town's respectable women. Luther's criticism of this rationale attacked his culture's gender presupposition concerning males. In asserting equal responsibility for males and females, Luther criticized the double standard of his day as well as the existence of brothels. Luther attempted to redefine his culture's understanding of male gender from uncontrollable impulse to social responsibility. Where the Reformation took root, brothels were outlawed.

For Luther, marriage and family life are Christian callings. His sermons and catechisms made it clear, in contrast to the theology and laws of the medieval church, that home and discipleship are not mutually exclusive. To the contrary, it is precisely in marriage that faithful sexual relations are possible, and religious vocation of loving the neighbor finds realization. To the medieval person, vocation was limited to priests, nuns, and monks. The thought that persons could serve God in marriage was revolutionary. Justification by grace alone, apart from works, liberated Christians from achieving salvation by renunciation of the world, and enabled service to the neighbor in the world. The neighbor here is the person encountered in the concrete situation, that is, parents, spouse, and children.

Luther rejected flight into self-chosen religious callings of clericalism, and called people to serve others in the web of relationships where they live. We are to do, Luther asserted, what God commands not what we fancy God would like. Here, again, Luther focused on the "the ordinary." The perennial temptation of the religious person is the desire to do "important" things rather than sweep the floor, change diapers, and do the dishes. Luther's point, however, is that we are not called to self-chosen extraordinary tasks, but rather to service in the world. Luther's ironic critique of medieval theology is evident in *The Estate of Marriage*:

> We err in that we judge the work of God according to our own feelings, and regard not his will but our own desire.... Now observe that when that clever harlot, our natural reason... takes a look at married life, she turns up her nose and says, "Alas, must I rock the baby, wash its diapers, make its bed, smell its stench, stay up nights with it, take care of it when it cries, heal its rashes and sores, and on top of that care for my wife, provide for her, labor at my trade, ... and whatever else of bitterness and drudgery married life involves? ... It is better to remain free and lead a peaceful, carefree life; I will become a priest or a nun and compel my children to do likewise."

For Luther, the Christian is called to love and serve others wherever God has placed him or her. Thus "when a father goes ahead and washes diapers or performs some other mean task for his child, and someone ridicules him as an effeminate fool...my dear fellow you tell me, which of the two is most keenly ridiculing the other? God, with all his angels and creatures is smiling – not because that father is washing diapers, but because he is doing so in Christian faith.''

A major social issue on the eve of the Reformation was widespread poverty exacerbated by the rapid, unrestrained growth of the profit economy and legitimated by the church's sanctification and idealization of poverty as the preferred condition of Christian life. Poverty was perceived as a kind of spiritual capital for poor and rich alike. The poor had a decided edge in the pilgrimage to salvation (the rich can no more squeeze through the eye of a needle into heaven than can a camel; Mark 10:25). On the other hand, the church had long emphasized that almsgiving atones for sin. Thus almsgiving provided the poor with some charity, enabled the rich to atone for their sins, and blessed the rich with the intercessions of the poor. The symbiotic relationship of rich and poor is succinctly expressed by the ancient line: "God could have made all men rich, but he wanted poor men in this world so that the rich might have an opportunity to redeem their sins.''

Luther's doctrine of justification cut the nerve of the medieval ideology of poverty. Since salvation is God's free gift, both poverty and almsgiving lose saving significance. The de-spiritualization of poverty allowed recognition of poverty as a personal and social evil to be combated. Justification by grace alone caused a paradigm shift in the understanding of poverty. Poverty was no longer understood as the favored status of the Christian, but rather a social ill to be combated. The poor are no longer the objects of meritorious charity, but neighbors to be served through justice and equity. Under the rubrics of justice and love to the neighbor, Luther and his colleagues moved in alliance with local governments to establish government welfare policies.

The first major effort was the Wittenberg Church Order of 1522 that established a "common chest" for welfare work. Initially funded by medieval ecclesiastical endowments and later by taxes, the Wittenberg Order prohibited begging; provided interest-free loans to artisans, who were to repay them whenever possible; provided for poor orphans, the children of poor people, and poor maidens who needed an appropriate dowry for marriage; provided refinancing of high interest loans at 4 percent annual interest for burdened citizens; and supported the education or vocational training of poor children. The Wittenberg common chest was a new creation of the Reformation that transformed theology into social praxis. Its financial basis soon included sales of grain, public collections, and a primitive banking operation. These resources enabled it to exercise a broad spectrum of social welfare including care of the sick and elderly and support of communal schools. Other communities quickly picked up these ideas. By 1523 the cities of Leisnig, Augsburg, Nuremberg, Altenburg, Kitzingen, Strasbourg, Breslau, and Regensburg had legislated common chest provisions for social welfare.

These ordinances for poor relief were efforts to implement Luther's conviction that social welfare policies designed to prevent as well as alleviate poverty are a Christian social responsibility. While Luther's efforts to develop welfare legislation were well received in the cities and territories that accepted the Reformation, his efforts to encourage civic control of capitalism gained little support. His conviction that Christian love is inseparable from equity and justice for the least in society ran into the stone wall of early modern capitalism. He discovered it was easier to motivate assistance to the poor than to curb the economic structures and practices that created and fostered the conditions of poverty. The squalor of poverty calls out for redress, whereas the attractive trappings of business muffle criticism. "How skillfully," Luther wrote,

"Sir Greed can dress up to look like a pious man if that seems to be what the occasion requires, while he is actually a double scoundrel and a liar."

Luther found the calculating entrepreneur extremely distasteful. He was convinced that the capitalist spirit divorced money from use for human needs and necessitated an economy of acquisition. Personal identity shifts from "you are who you love" to "you are what you have." From his *Sermon on Usury* (1519) to his *Admonition to the Clergy that they Preach Against Usury* (1540), Luther consistently preached and wrote against the expanding money and credit economy as a great sin. In the latter tract, he wrote: "After the devil there is no greater human enemy on earth than a miser and usurer, for he desires to be above everyone. Turks, soldiers, and tyrants are also evil men, yet they allow the people to live. . . . But a usurer and miser-belly desires that the whole world be ruined in order that there be hunger, thirst, misery, and need so that he can have everything and so that everyone must depend upon him and be his slave as if he were God."

Such usury, Luther argued, affects everyone. "The usury which occurs in Leipzig, Augsburg, Frankfurt, and other comparable cities is felt in our market and our kitchen. The usurers are eating our food and drinking our drink." By manipulating prices "usury lives off the bodies of the poor." "The world is one big whorehouse, completely submerged in greed," where the "big thieves hang the little thieves" and the big fish eat the little fish. Thus Luther exhorted pastors to condemn usury as stealing and murder, and to refuse absolution and the sacrament to usurers unless they repent.

Luther's concern was not only about an individual's use of money, but also the structural social damage inherent in the idolatry of the "laws" of the market. Ideas of an "impersonal market" and "autonomous laws of economics" were abhorrent to Luther because he saw them as both idolatrous and socially destructive. He saw the community endangered by the rising financial power of a few great economic centers; their unregulated economic coercion would destroy the ethos of the community. To Luther early capitalism was doubly dangerous because it not only exploited people but also strove to conceal its voracious nature and to deceive people.

Throughout his career Luther fought against what he saw as the two-sided coin of mammonism: ascetic flight from money and the acquisitive drive for it. His foundation for this battle was the great reversal of the gospel that a person's worth is not determined by what he or she does or does not possess, but rather by God's promise in Christ. Thus money is not the lord of life, but the gift of God for serving the neighbor and building up the community. Luther believed that the church was called publicly and unequivocally to reject exploitative economic developments, and to develop a constructive social ethic in response to them. This social ethic contributed directly to the enactment of social welfare legislation in areas that accepted the Reformation, and called for public accountability of large business through government regulation. In his *Commentary on Psalm 82*, Luther argued that the government "is to help the poor, the orphans, and the widows to justice, and to further their cause [through regulation of business].... For where there are no laws, the poor, the widows, and the orphans are oppressed.... And this is equally true of buying, selling, inheriting, lending, paying, borrowing, and the like. It is only a matter of one getting the better of another, robbing him, stealing from him, and cheating him. This happens most of all to the poor, the widows, and the orphans."

Luther understood his task as theologian and preacher is to provide a clear critique of existing social structures, and to call the community to work in the different "estates" for the well being of the neighbor and the common good. For Luther and his colleagues this meant that faith active in love to the neighbor is incarnated not only through the web of social relationships rooted in marriage and family, but also through government legislation for the common good.

Other Reformers shared these perspectives on love. For example, the Dominican monk Martin Bucer (1491–1551) was resident in the Heidelberg monastery when Luther gave his "Heidelberg Disputation." Bucer went on to become a Reformer in his own right, first in Strasbourg and then in Cambridge. It was in Strasbourg that Bucer wrote his own tract on love, translated as *Instruction in Christian Love* (1523), in response to requests that he state and account for his faith. The long German title of this tract literally reads: "That no one should live for himself but for others, and how man can attain that ideal." It has been suggested that Bucer took his title from the concluding section of Luther's *The Freedom of a Christian*: "We conclude, therefore, that a Christian lives not in himself, but in Christ and in his neighbor. . . . He lives in Christ through faith, in his neighbor through love."

Indeed, *The Freedom of a Christian* became a classic in its own time with its opening theses: "A Christian is a perfectly free lord of all, subject to none. A Christian is a perfectly dutiful servant of all, subject to all." Luther continued: "These two theses seem to contradict each other. If, however, they should be found to fit together they would serve our purpose beautifully. Both are Paul's own statements, who says in I Cor. 9[:19], 'For though I am free from all men, I have made myself a slave to all,' and in Rom. 13[:8], 'Owe no one anything, except to love one another.' Love by its very nature is ready to serve and be subject to him who is loved."

Chapter 9

Love as Service: Pietism and the Diaconal Movements

Nearly a century after Luther penned *The Freedom of a Christian*, the most popular devotional book in the history of Western Christianity, *Sechs Bücher vom wahren Christenthum* (*True Christianity*) echoed his theses: "What is a Christian according to faith but namely a lord over everything; and what is he according to love but namely a servant among everyone." Johann Arndt's (1555–1621) *True Christianity* began with "book one" in 1605 and was completed posthumously with a length of about 1,000 pages – saturated with discussion and meditation on love. While the phrasing of Luther's and Arndt's theses is nearly identical, their respective contexts differed. As Wallmann notes, Arndt's pastoral ministry was addressed to "the changed situation of the third post-Reformation generation." The late medieval person tormented by guilt and the efforts to overcome it by good works found liberation in Luther's proclamation of justification by grace alone apart from works. Arndt's audience in the post-Reformation context had grown accustomed to hearing of the graceful God who forgives sin, but Arndt did not see the fruits of this faith. As Heinrich Heine (1797–1856), the German Romantic poet, reputedly said on his deathbed, "Of course God will forgive me; that's his job." Centuries later, the martyr to National Socialism, Dietrich Bonhoeffer (1906–1945) called this "cheap grace." Hence Arndt's opening sentence of the first edition of *True Christianity*: "The reason for this little book was given to me by the great and shameful abuse of the dear gospel, the great impenitence and security of the people who praise Christ and his holy gospel with full mouths and never-theless with their works behave and act contrary to the gospel just as if they had renounced the gospel." "Where," Arndt asked, "is brotherly love?"

Faith, Arndt did not tire of asserting, is to be active in love for love is rooted in faith. "Faith unites with God, love with humankind." "The love of God and the neighbor is one, and must not be divided. True godly love cannot be better noted and proved than by love of the neighbor." "God extends his love over all humankind, which he attests to not only in his Word but also in all of nature." Sun, air, water, earth are for all – the highest and lowest. And as God intends for us, so we should intend for our neighbor. God does not need our service, but our neighbor does. "For so strong is the commandment of love to the neighbor that if it is broken then God's love is withdrawn from us, and the person is immediately judged and condemned by the strict righteousness of God." "If you hate your brother, then you hate God who has forbidden such." True worship is nothing other than to serve the neighbor with love and good deeds. Such love is pure when one loves the neighbor not for the sake of one's own need and enjoyment, but purely for the sake of God because God has so loved us. Why ought you love your enemy? Because God commands it. Echoing Luther's comment that the heart creates its gods, Arndt wrote: "The human heart is thus created by God so that it cannot live without love. It must love something, whether it be God, the world, or the self." The entire book is concerned with true and false love and how to serve God and the neighbor.

To cite Wallmann again, "Arndt's desire was to lead Christians to *true godliness* (*pietas*). He turned against a spreading ungodliness (*impietas*) among Christians. He was not directed against a theoretical atheism, which in fact did not yet exist in his time, but against the practical atheism which confessed Christ only with the mouth but not with the heart and that denied him in fact." As we shall see, by the mid-nineteenth century when atheism had arrived, Ludwig Feuerbach (1804–1872) – famous or infamous as the case may be for his claim that theology is really anthropology – chided Christians for their "practical atheism" that gave lip service to God but neglected love to the neighbor.

In 1675 an edition of Arndt's extremely popular and frequently republished sermons appeared with a new preface written by Philipp Jakob Spener (1635–1705). The preface caused such a sensation that it was reprinted independently within months with the title *Pia Desideria* (*Pious Desires*), and became the programmatic text for a renewal movement that soon came to be known as Pietism. While Spener at that time was a Lutheran pastor in Frankfurt, Pietism intentionally transcended denominations and national borders for its orientation was to the practice of Christianity; the emphasis was upon love inseparable from faith. Spener emphasized "it is by no means enough to have knowledge of the Christian faith, for Christianity consists rather of practice." The mark of this practice is love. "Indeed, love is the whole life of man who has faith and who through his faith is saved, and his fulfillment of the laws of God consists of love." "Fervent love . . . toward all men," including "unbelievers and heretics" will accomplish, he wrote, "all that we desire."

In the context of bitter post-Reformation disputes not only between Protestants and Catholics but among Protestants concerning who is theologically correct, Spener argued that "disputing is not enough either to maintain the truth among ourselves or to impart it to the erring. The holy love of God is necessary. If only we Evangelicals would make it our serious business to offer God the fruits of his truth in fervent love, ... and show this in recognizable and unalloyed love of our neighbors, including those who are heretics...." Spener's appeal to love over conflict gains added significance when we remember that he was writing less than a generation after the close of one of the most devastating wars on European soil, the Thirty Years' War (1618–1648), itself rooted in religious conflict. Accompanying social disasters included famine, plague, class conflict, and growing criticism of the church, all of which fed into what Beyreuther referred to as a widespread secret atheism.

In this context Spener proclaimed hope for a better time, and in his pastorates in Frankfurt, Berlin, and elsewhere strove to live out the practice of love he proclaimed. The burdens of the poor, he wrote, are a "blot on our Christianity," and necessitate rethinking our own property in terms of the common good. Thus he became active in the development of poor relief efforts in those two major cities. As leader of the Frankfurt clergy he dismissed haphazard almsgiving as ineffective and reconceived the city's poor relief. His work on social welfare brought him widespread attention and in 1693 Elector Friedrich III requested his advice on alleviating the dire social problems of Berlin. The city had nearly doubled in size to some 50,000 within one generation and included a large number of discharged soldiers and the widows and orphans of fallen soldiers. Spener's response was that support be provided through the creation of employment offices and public institutions for the humane care for invalids, widows, and orphans without regard to their person and religious affiliation. Financing was provided by the city parliament through weekly house-to-house collections; the state provided a subsidy to the discharged soldiers. The administration of the work- and poorhouses was assigned to 12 committees of elected citizens under the supervision of both Berlin provosts. The Elector created a central poor relief fund in 1695. Institutions for the poor, the sick, and orphans soon followed. In quick succession similar institutions were developed in many German locales.

Spener's concern to develop social implementations of God's love was energetically pursued by one of his most dedicated followers, August Hermann Francke (1663–1727). While preparing for parish ministry, Francke went through a severe crisis of faith followed by a conversion experience that charted the rest of his life. Now certain of God's existence and his own spiritual rebirth, he became a pastor in Glaucha, an economically and socially depressed suburb of Halle, the site of the new Prussian University of Halle. Francke's theological orientation was to emphasize continual growth in faith and improvement of life. The converted person was to be continually zealous in overcoming sin and diligent in doing good. Where such marks are not evident, "it is," he wrote, "a certain and clear sign that the life which is from God is no longer in him. For where it is in the person, there is no standing still but rather continual advance and perpetual growth."

"Perpetual growth" was certainly the characteristic of Francke's life and work. Through Spener's influence he received an academic post at Halle University as Professor of Oriental Languages along with his pastoral position in Glaucha. He initiated and throughout his life was the moving force behind institutions he centered at Halle. These included an orphanage, training schools for teachers and pastors, various schools for different levels and classes of students, a center for the study and translation of the Bible, a publishing house, science laboratory, and apothecary. He titled his account of these developments *Die Fussstapfen des noch lebenden Gottes*

(*Footprints of the Still-Living God*). This classic defense of Pietism and social activism was printed in English as *Pietas Hallensis,* and strongly influenced the British Isles and then developments in American colonies.

In many respects Francke was a modern entrepreneur. He initiated these institutions with only the small amount of money he found in his parish poor box, and they became the imposing series of Baroque buildings still standing at Halle University. He was also modern in arranging these institutions. He separated the orphanage from the poorhouse, the workhouse, and the house of correction. The orphanage was the most advanced of the time. Among other things it was a pioneer in hygiene. At a time when no one took offence at bodily uncleanness, Francke and his colleagues insisted that the children in their charge brush their teeth, bathe, and have clean clothes and bedding. Here cleanliness, as John Wesley affirmed, was indeed next to godliness.

The university became a center for theology students whose studies were related directly to practice, for example work in the hospital and knowledge of pharmaceuticals. Francke fostered such studies with the motto that a Christian "shall be equipped and sent out so that all the world may see that no more useful people may be found than those who belong to Jesus Christ." Francke placed great value upon the fruits of love as signs of living faith. His energetic efforts on behalf of the poor and marginalized expressed his understanding of who the neighbor is and how to love him or her. The Halle programs were also conceived and perceived as expressions of the credibility of faith active in love in social and economic activism.

Care for the sick and poor among Roman Catholics had its modern roots in the work of St. Vincent de Paul (1581–1660) who is remembered not only for his own efforts to apply Christian love to social issues but also for founding the Sisters of Charity (1633), the first Roman Catholic congregation of women devoted entirely to care of the sick and poor. A major lay association arose with the leadership of Frédéric Ozanam in Paris in 1833 – the Society of St. Vincent de Paul. ''Caritas'' organizations, beginning in Freiburg, Germany in 1897, soon spread throughout the world. These national movements came under the umbrella of Caritas Internationalis in 1957. The influence of De Paul and also the Sisters of Charity stimulated a number of Protestant leaders – women and men – in their own efforts to relate love to pressing social concerns.

The application of love to social and economic issues became increasingly difficult for both Protestants and Roman Catholics in the generations following Francke. The Enlightenment challenge to faith, to be picked up in our next chapter, was but one of the tests put to those who believed faith to be active in love. The late eighteenth century witnessed widespread famines, epidemics, homelessness, unemployment, and underemployment. Ten percent of the German population was forced to survive through begging. The nineteenth century began with the storm and consequences of the French Revolution (1789) with its enthusiasms, but the Napoleonic wars and the development of factories also contributed to personal and social suffering and demoralization. Responses came from individuals – including women – across the spectrum of churches and countries. The English Quaker, Elizabeth Fry (1780–1845), mother of 11 children, began her ministry of love in London's infamous Newgate prison, and by 1817 had formed the ''Association of Women for Female Prisoners.'' She became a leading advocate for prison reform and against the death penalty under her motto, ''punishment ought not be vengeance.'' At home she became an inspiration to Florence Nightingale (1820–1910), and abroad she lectured in Berlin, Bremen, and Hanover. The pioneer of women's service in Germany was Amalie Sieveking (1794–1859), who during the 1831 cholera epidemic in Hamburg called upon women in the name of Christ to care for the sick. She called on women for assistance to serve "the poorest and the weakest" "as far as our influence can reach with the heavenly power of love."

The most successful recruitment of Protestant women for service to the marginalized came through the work of Theodor Fliedner (1800–1864), pastor of a struggling parish in Kaiserswerth on the Rhine. In his travels to raise funds for local needs he visited England five times where he became acquainted with Elisabeth Fry as well as the industrial development taking place there. At home he unsuccessfully appealed for the establishment of an asylum for released women prisoners, and thus began the work himself in his own home. By 1836 he and his wife had opened a school for young children and an institute to train women in nursing. These "deaconesses" as Fliedner now called them attracted more and more young women to service as Christian nurses, including Florence Nightingale who spent time studying at Kaiserswerth. The deaconess movement spread throughout Europe and into the Near East. In the process of training and serving these women not only brought healing and hope to the marginalized, they also pioneered the way toward the emancipation of women from the dominant view of the time that limited women to the home.

Another social reformer of the time was Johann Hinrich Wichern (1808–1881), who referred to Vincent de Paul as "unmatched" in the world for his love to the poor. Born in Hamburg during the French occupation, by 15 Wichern became responsible for his six younger siblings and mother upon the death of his father. Yet with incredible drive and the assistance of his deceased father's friends he gained a university education in theology. Wichern's visit to the Francke institutions in Halle impressed him and reinforced his openness to contemporary calls for prison reform and support for the poor. In 1831 he became an assistant to a Hamburg pastor, Rautenberg, who was influenced by the English proposals for Sunday Schools that would provide learning and moral instruction to poor children.

Wichern recorded his shocked descriptions of the living conditions of the urban proletariat in his diary, and his early writings parallel Friedrich Engels' descriptions of the situation of the English working class. The young Wichern used large parish meetings as a bully pulpit to challenge citizens to charitable work. Convinced that neglected and abused children had to be given a new environment, he gained access to a dilapidated cottage on a local estate and began a rescue home for children. Known as the "Rauhe Haus" ("Rough House") because of its poor condition, but called by Wichern "the House of Love," he, his mother, a sister and brother, moved in and began repairs. Within days they were bringing in neglected children of the city. By the end of the year (1833) there were 12 boys ranging in age from five to eighteen most of whom Wichern had met in prison or on the streets where they literally spent their nights. One of the 12-year-olds had been arrested 92 times for theft!

Wichern noted that the power of sin needs no demonstration but love does. He told the children he knew their pasts, but that they were now forgiven. In addition to forgiveness, he emphasized trust as the avenue to creating a new life. Thus he removed fences and locks, and stated there would be no spying. In spite of thefts and runaways, Wichern held to his vision that liberation from sin led to human freedom and love. As the children who remained gained in experience of freedom, mutual responsibility, and care for each other, the home expanded. By 1839, it was clear that Wichern needed more help for the Rauhe Haus, and he established a "Bruderhaus" to train others in the service of love. This was the beginning of a male diaconate. He saw a fundamental need for the development of a community that would train future educators and co-workers in the church's works of love.

The context for so much social misery was the beginning of the industrial age. There were no laws protecting workers or regulating their work other than the 1839 Prussian law that prohibited children under nine from factory labor, and that children were not to work at night, on Sunday, and no more than ten hours a day. People came to the cities in search of work and multiplied the industrial proletariat, most of whom worked for starvation wages and lived in overcrowded, terrible conditions. Friedrich Engels, the close associate of Karl Marx, knew these conditions firsthand from his youth in a worker family of Wuppertal. He saw on Sundays the pious factory owners and supervisors go to church while their workers barely eked out their lives. Wichern, too, understood the spiritual and material conditions of these workers, and sought to alleviate those conditions through the work of his deacons, a work he referred to as the "Inner Mission." The point of the Inner Mission was that the church's missionary work also needed to address the loss of faith and social injustices of Europe.

Wichern's work became increasingly known throughout Germany, creating state and church rescue homes for thousands of orphans. By 1844 he was publishing his own paper with articles on the social needs of the day, reports on the churches, and works of love in order to strengthen the consciousness of solidarity and fellowship in service. He was optimistic that "the spirit of compassionate love is again awakened in [the Christian community]. This has opened and confirmed the Kingdom of God upon earth as a kingdom of saving love in Christ." The Kingdom of God, however, was understood differently by many of his contemporaries. In the flux of the political, social, and economic issues leading up to 1848 – the year of revolutions and the "Communist Manifesto" – many

socialists were ripe for a utopian classless society while many
of the liberal bourgeoisie continued to be addicted to dreams of
a technological utopia to which the present social pain was
rationalized as the midwife.

Eventually aware that events were passing them by, the
churches called for an all-German church meeting in 1848 in
Wittenberg, the first Kirchentag. As they met, barricades were
being manned in Berlin. Wichern attended on the condition
that he might speak on behalf of the Inner Mission. After
endless debates on the state of the church and nation, Wichern
asserted that the issue of the Inner Mission must be taken up.
His entire speech was impromptu, and there is only the steno-
grapher's recorded text. He noted that people should not be
surprised that the unprecedented has happened; they should
have seen it coming in the oppressive conditions foisted upon
the proletariat. The Inner Mission, he said, had long warned of
the abyss that now lay unmasked before them. The people no
longer go to the church, therefore the church must go to the
people. "My friends! It is necessary that the whole church
recognize this: The work of the Inner Mission is mine! The
church must place its seal on the sum total of this work: Love
belongs to me as much as faith. Saving love must become the
great instrument by which the church manifests the fact of its
faith. This love must flame up in the church as the bright torch
of God, making Christ known in his people. As the whole
Christ reveals himself in the living Word of God, so he must
proclaim himself also in divine deeds, and the highest, purest,
most churchly of these deeds is redeeming love."

Wichern was overjoyed by the Assembly's positive response
to take up the cause of the Inner Mission. But as Beyreuther
notes, Wichern did not remain free of the "catastrophe
psychosis" of 1848 that affected the bourgeoisie. He saw
the revolution as an atheistic uprising because he associated
it so closely to Communism. The dramatic opening of the

Communist Manifesto – "A specter covers Europe, the specter of Communism" – fueled fears of an anarchistic and atheistic proletariat. At the same time, Wichern's theological perspective was a strength as well as a weakness. For him, the first step to the reform of society was repentance by everyone, including the working class. He conceived of the social order as viable with reform, whereas Marx believed the society was determined by class conflict and the church had outlived its usefulness. Whereas Wichern saw the origins of social and economic suffering in the "de-Christianization" of society, Marx saw them in the bourgeois method of production blessed by the church and state. Thus to the Communists and other social revolutionaries, the principle of "saving love" only stood in the way of a revolutionary ushering in of a classless society. The efforts of state and church to overcome mass need through a social policy on work and the economy was too little and too late.

Echoes of Wichern's call for "saving love" may, however, be heard in the turn-of-the-century Evangelical Social Congress that provided Protestant intellectuals and theologians a platform for their goal of establishing a modern welfare state. Its president for many years was the famous historian of dogma, Adolf von Harnack (1851–1920). On the Roman Catholic side there was Leo XIII's (1810–1903) encyclical "Rerum Novarum" (1891) that advocated social justice, especially with regard to working conditions. In America, "saving love" took the form of the Social Gospel movement that also promoted in words and actions the inseparability of love and justice. One of its leading exponents, Walter Rauschenbusch (1861–1918) whose first parish ministry was in "Hell's Kitchen," New York City, was a tireless advocate for social justice.

In his *Dare We Be Christians?* Rauschenbusch wrote concerning the class conflicts related to industrialization. "The gravest issue is not simply a question of dollars and cents, but of the sterilization of love by social injustice. If love is really as important to God and humanity as we have said, this social antagonism becomes a very serious thing to a religious mind. Must we permanently live in a loveless industrial world, or do we dare to be Christians?"

Among the many influenced by Rauschenbusch were Reinhold Niebuhr and Martin Luther King, Jr. (1929–1968). Niebuhr (1892–1971) gave a sharper, more realistic focus with his view of justice as an "approximation of brotherhood under conditions of sin," and advocated political policies that recognized the sharp distinction between "moral man and immoral society." In King's _Strength to Love_ he has a chapter that is an imaginary letter from St. Paul to American Christians in which he writes: "I must say to you ... that love is the most durable power in the world. Throughout the centuries men have sought to discover the highest good.... This was one of the big questions of Greek philosophy. The Epicureans and the Stoics sought to answer it; Plato and Aristotle sought to answer it. What is the _summum bonum_ of life? I think I have found the answer, America. I have discovered that the highest good is love. This principle is at the centre of the cosmos. It is the great unifying force of life. God is love. He who loves has discovered the clue to the meaning of ultimate reality; he who hates stands in immediate candidacy for nonbeing."

Chapter 10

Love in the Modern World

Love in the modern world took a number of trajectories. While Wichern and others were striving to respond to the social and economic challenges of their day, their colleagues in philosophy and theology were responding to the intellectual challenges posed by the rise of the sciences, both natural and social. Meanwhile, writers of novels, poetry, plays, and operas were luxuriating in a public market that could not get enough love-stories.

The discovery of religion as a historical human phenomenon, Enlightenment philosophy, and the developing natural scientific method began severely eroding the traditional foundations of religion. If Christianity, and thus its contributions to the understandings and expressions of love, were to survive it would be, according to Immanuel Kant (1724–1804), a *Religion within the Limits of Reason Alone*. Kant challenged his contemporaries to think for themselves, "have the courage to make use of your own understanding." The courageous person dares to become autonomous. By this, Kant did not mean do whatever you want but rather emancipation from every form of heteronomy, from all laws external to oneself be they parental, societal, ecclesiastical, or religious. True autonomy is "self-law" in obedience to the universal law of reason. Love as an affect therefore cannot be commanded, but love understood in Kant's terms as the "categorical imperative" (acting on that principle that could be a universal law governing everyone's actions) can be commanded. If you ought, Kant famously stated, then you can.

Duty and reason, however, proved an unsatisfying diet to the succeeding generation. Kant's disinterested benevolence held no promise of bliss for the reaction to the Enlightenment known as Romanticism. The "disenchantment of the world," as Max Weber so famously described the effect of philosophy and science, had to be countered by the re-enchantment of the world through love. That was the self-appointed task of Romanticism. Romanticism is notoriously difficult to define; perhaps its elusiveness is due to its yearning for individual fulfillment that always appeared one step beyond realization. The dynamic power in Romanticism is the conviction that the infinite is present in the finite but that no particular form can contain it. We noticed this dynamic in the Greek eros – and it is probably no accident that this is the period of new appreciation and translation of Plato. The Romantic eros now is not merely directed vertically in ascent, but horizontally as well. The infinite is not only above, it is ahead promising new possibilities. The downside of this perspective is that the infinite also extends down into the demonic depths of the soul. Hence, the "father" of existentialism, Søren Kierkegaard (1813–1855) coined the concept of "angst" and penned *The Concept of Dread* and *The Sickness Unto Death*.

Kierkegaard also gave voice to the corollary of the Romantic eros in his *The Concept of Irony*. Tillich discusses the Romantic sense of "irony" as the superiority of the infinite to every finite expression, driving beyond each finite expression to another.

The ego is thus free from bondage to concrete situations whether they are the forms of faith, personal relationships, or the various sociological forms of family, church, and politics. Irony may be used to reveal that what was believed to be reality is not that reality. Irony can be a disruptive force with the power to undo texts and readers alike. Within Romanticism there is an ironical elevation of the individual beyond his or her situation in life. In the *Athenaeum Fragments*, Friedrich Schlegel (1772–1829), one of the leaders of the Romantic Movement, emphasized becoming over being: The "true essence" of Romantic is "that it is always in the process of becoming and can never be completed." "[I]t alone is free and recognizes as its first law that the poetic will submits itself to no other law." While this had a certain exhilarating liberation in questioning communal standards, it could also lead to a sense of emptiness by eroding tradition, beliefs, and ethics. Such a consequence occurred with Schlegel himself who converted to Roman Catholicism in search of an authoritative system with given content and form.

Similarly, Schlegel's friend Novalis (Friedrich von Hardenberg, 1772–1801), who according to Barth "represents in a uniquely pure way the intentions and achievements of this entire group [of Romantic writers]," was leaning toward Roman Catholicism by the end of his short life. Novalis' poem "Hymns to the Night" expressed his passion and grief over the early death at 15 of his fiancée, Sophie von Kühn. He himself died soon afterward from tuberculosis at the age of 29. His major unfinished writing, a critique of the Enlightenment ideal of reason and utilitarianism, was *Heinrich von Ofterdingen*, a fairy tale of a young medieval poet who searches for the mysterious blue flower of his dream. The "blue flower," becoming a central symbol of Romanticism, stood for desire, love; a longing for home and a longing for the infinite. In the course of Heinrich's search, he finds that the blue flower is the maiden Matilda who reveals to him the metaphysical power of love fundamental for the redemption of the world and its transition into the golden age. Heinrich, the hero of the novel, is based upon a historical figure, a medieval troubadour. Here the romantic idealization of the Middle Ages is both the poetic counter to the Enlightenment and the transitional period to the golden age when the self will be in All and All in the self; nature, self, and spirit will be one.

The means to this transition is woman. Romantics idolized female subjectivity – women are their muses. Life is exalted through ardent fantasy; fairy tales and poetry. Heinrich senses immortality through Matilda: "Of what use is a spirit without a heaven to dwell in? and you are the heaven that upholds and supports me. . . . I cannot comprehend eternity except through my love for you. We are eternal because we love." Novalis affirmed love to be the primal foundation of the universe: "Love is the goal of the world's history – the Amen of the universe." The languages of love and religion become interchangeable. "'O beloved, heaven has given you to me to worship. I pray to you, you are the saint who carries my wishes to the ear of God, through whom he reveals himself to me, through whom he declares to me the abundance of his love. What is religion but an unlimited understanding, an eternal union of loving hearts? . . . You are . . . eternal life in most alluring guise . . . I swear to be yours eternally, Matilda, as truly as love, God's presence, is with us.'" Novalis influenced generations of German writers including Rainer Maria Rilke, Hermann Hesse, and Thomas Mann.

Baumer notes that the romantics talked freely and at length about the unconscious. "The unconscious was used to explain not only the creative process but also the 'night side' of human life, the world of dreams, monsters, and apparitions. In dreams the soul, precisely because it is withdrawn from sense impressions, has contact with divine reality, thus enabling the

'hidden poet' in man to emerge." For Heinrich von Ofterdingen, dreams are "heavenly gifts" which rend the veil of
our inward nature and guide us "in our pilgrimage to the holy
tomb." Love in the dramas of the genre was a primitive
unconscious force, sweeping people away by elemental passions. But this may be a two-edged sword for dreams can
also be nightmares, revealing not only "heavenly gifts" but
demonic forces. Such a nightmarish quality appears in some of
Francisco Goya's (1746–1828) art where frightful apparitions
rise from the depths of the unconscious. In his well-known
engraving "The Dream of Reason Produces Monsters" reason
forsakes man. Edvard Munch's (1863–1944) "The Scream,"
before its banalization on T-shirts, was also shocking. And his
erotic "Madonna" with its original framing by sperms and
skulls depicts the old theme of the intimate relationship of
eros and *thanatos*, love and death. That great exponent of
the power of negative thinking Arthur Schopenhauer (1788–
1860) posited that in this worst of all possible worlds there
is a worm in every apple, and humankind is propelled by
its heartless and egoist will to survive. The dark side of eros is
seen in Schopenhauer's blind "will to live" (*The World as Will
and Idea*, 1818). Humankind's endless striving only creates
suffering and strife, and reveals love as delusional and
illusional.

The Romantic yearning for the Infinite like the ancient and
medieval imagery of ascent expresses the Platonic Eros. In this
context, Schlegel initiated a critical German translation of
Plato with Friedrich Schleiermacher (1768–1834), one of the
most influential theologians between the Reformation and the
twentieth century. At the time, Schleiermacher was a young
pastor in Berlin. Berlin was rapidly becoming the hub of
German Romanticism, and Schleiermacher soon joined one
of the renowned literary circles, the salon of Henrietta Herz,
that included Friedrich Schlegel. After Schlegel abandoned the

Plato translation project, Schleiermacher completed it, and it remains a landmark of Plato scholarship.

The Romantic endorsement of passion over convention was scandalously promoted in Schlegel's *Lucinde* (1799), a somewhat incoherent praise of romantic love and marriage as the encounter with the divine source of life. In contrast to the "mere concubinage" and "slavery" of bourgeois marriage, the Romantics stressed women's individuality and freedom. Schleiermacher's own relationships with women became "a matter," in the words of Clements, "which has by turns embarrassed and intrigued his biographers and commentators." His close friendship with Henrietta Herz was a source of Berlin gossip though they both maintained their mutual attraction was intellectual and spiritual. A more tumultuous relationship was with Eleonore Grunow, the unhappily married wife of a fellow Berlin pastor. Schleiermacher began courting her soon after they met in 1799. Clements states that their relationship was "virtually a secret betrothal." Schleiermacher hoped his urging that she would divorce her husband would lead to their marriage. After some years of indecision, however, she decided to remain in her marriage. Redeker states: "Schleiermacher held the view that in marriage every woman had an inalienable right to her own individuality. This romantic conception of individuality was for him in agreement with the view that a marriage in which a woman is prevented by the moral unworthiness of the other partner from developing her own individuality is no longer a marriage but a subversion of mankind's holiest bonds. Therefore, he considered it his duty to dissolve such a marriage which was really no marriage." He later reversed his view and believed marriage is indissoluble.

Schleiermacher's literary contribution to the salon set was *On Religion: Speeches to its Cultured Despisers* (1799). *On Religion* argues that the cultured of his day reject religion for the wrong reasons; they mistake externals for essence. Rational analysis of religion is not equivalent to understanding and feeling religion. "The members and juices of an organized body can be dissected; but take these elements now and mix them and treat them in every possible way; and will you be able to make heart's blood of them? Once dead, can it ever again move in a living body?" In short, after the frog has visited the biology lab he loses his "frogness." In order to understand the world and religion, Schleiermacher argued, one "must first have found humanity, and he finds it only in and through love." Religion is "the immediate feeling of the Infinite and Eternal" not some utilitarian or higher hedonism aimed at eternal rewards. Religion is not a system of theory or morality; rather religion is "feeling," "an immediate self-consciousness."

The Romantic themes of yearning, feeling, intuition, and irony may be seen in Schleiermacher's "Second Speech" where he speaks of the human "endeavor to return into the Whole, and to exist for oneself at the same time.... How now are you in the Whole? By your senses. And how are you for yourselves? By the unity of your self-consciousness, which is given chiefly in the possibility of comparing the varying degrees of sensation." He then describes the nature of religious experience in erotic terms.

> [I]t is bashful and tender as a maiden's kiss, it is holy and fruitful as a bridal embrace. Nor is it merely like, it is all this. It is the first contact of the universal life with an individual.
>
> ... It is the holy wedlock of the Universe with the incarnated Reason for a creative, productive embrace.... You lie directly on the bosom of the infinite world. In that moment, you are its soul. Through one part of your nature you feel, as your own, all its powers and its endless life. In that moment it is your body, you pervade, as your own, its muscles and members and your thinking and forecasting set its inmost nerves in motion. In this way every living, original movement in your life is first received.

A reorientation to the theological concept of love came with Ludwig Feuerbach (1804–1872), whose works were influential upon numerous modern thinkers including Karl Marx (1818–1883), Friedrich Engels (1820–1895), and foreshadowed both Martin Buber's (1878–1965) *I and Thou*, and Sigmund Freud's (1856–1939) *The Future of an Illusion*. Feuerbach went to study theology at the University of Heidelberg where he was soon convinced that philosophy had much more to offer than "the web of sophisms" he heard from his professor.

Feuerbach's most famous work, *The Essence of Christianity*, appeared in 1841 and immediately created a furor about his theory of religion as projection. Christianity (he later extended his theory to all religions) is the projection of human fears, hopes, and love which then are labeled God. In short, as he famously asserted: "Theology is anthropology." "Religion, at least the Christian, is the relation of man to himself, . . . The divine being is nothing else than the human being, or, rather, the human nature purified, freed from the limits of the individual. . . . All the attributes of the divine nature are, therefore, attributes of the human nature." "The personality of God is nothing else than the projected personality of man" "freed from all the conditions and limitations of Nature." Having gained his contemporaries' attention, Feuerbach went on to assert that to negate the subject – God – does not mean to negate the predicates (wisdom, love, justice). The real atheist, he insisted, is the person who theoretically acknowledges God and lives as if God did not exist; that is, lives without love.

The praise of love pervades *The Essence of Christianity*.

> It was love to which God sacrificed his divine majesty. And what sort of love was that? another than ours? . . . Was it the love of himself? . . . No! it was love to man. But is not love to man human love? Can I love man without loving him

humanly, without loving him as he himself loves, if he truly loves? Would not love be otherwise a devilish love? The devil too loves man, but not for man's sake – for his own; thus he loves man out of egotism, to aggrandize himself, to extend his power. But God loves man for man's sake, i.e., that he may make him good, happy, blessed.... For though there is also a self-interested love among men, still the true human love, which alone is worthy of the name, is that which impels the sacrifice of self to another.

In this sense "religion is man's consciousness of himself in his concrete or living totality, in which the identity of self-consciousness exists only as the pregnant complete unity of *I* and *thou*." Our neighbor is not an "it" to be used but a person, a "thou." "The other is my *thou*,... In another I first have the consciousness of humanity;... in my love to him it is clear to me that he belongs to me and I to him, that we two cannot be without each other, that only community constitutes humanity."

The humanness of love is revealed in the family. "The highest and deepest love is the mother's love." "Love is in and by itself essentially feminine in nature. The belief in the love of God is the belief in the feminine principle as divine. Love apart from living nature is an anomaly, a phantom." "Love especially works wonders, and the love of the sexes most of all. Man and woman are the complement of each other, and thus united they first present the species, the perfect man.... [I]n love, man declares himself unsatisfied in his individuality taken by itself, he postulates the existence of another as a need of the heart; he reckons another as part of his own being; he declares the life which he has through love to be the truly human life...."

We might describe Feuerbach's project to be the description of God as a creative fiction to enable the liberation of a creative love in both agapaic and erotic forms for the "thou."

In contrast, we might describe the work of Friedrich Nietzsche (1844–1900) to be the description of God as a destructive fiction to enable a destructive love that attacks humankind by suppressing the erotic will to power in favor of the weakest members of the species. Nietzsche, educated at the universities of Bonn and Leipzig became a professor of classical philology at the Swiss University of Basel. Lonely and in perpetual poor health, Nietzsche resigned his post in 1879. His writings were largely ignored until the end of his life, but by then he had suffered a complete mental breakdown and died insane. It is of interest that his well known work, *Die fröhliche Wissenschaft* (*The Gay Science*, 1882, wherein he proclaimed the death of God) was inspired by the songs of the troubadours, and that its reissue added an appendix of songs echoing those of the troubadours. From his study of Greek philosophy, Nietzsche developed his "Dionysian" theme of transforming the tragedy of life through withstanding and thereby transforming suffering. So in *Thus Spake Zarathustra*, Nietzsche stated: "I should only believe in a God that would know how to dance." Dionysius, the god of life-affirming joy, of erotic will to power should displace Jesus, the god of decadent love for the weak who ought to be eliminated. The will to power, i.e., the will to life, to self-affirmation, is *Beyond Good and Evil*. Those who successfully pursue and realize power are "supermen," a thesis he pursues in *On the Geneology of Morals*. Christian love, agape, is antithetical to Nietzsche's ideal because self-giving or sacrificing love is the impotent morality of slaves who resent the strong and project revenge in terms of heaven and hell. That is why Christianity appealed to the marginalized of the Roman Empire who could only adopt a "slave morality" in contrast to "master morality." Feelings of guilt, the "bad conscience," are the results of the unhealthy Christian morality that thwarts our natural inclinations. His disdain for Christianity was one of the reasons for his break with his one-time close friend

Richard Wagner (1813–1883), whose *Parsifal* Nietzsche considered a hypocritical obeisance to Christianity.

Nietzsche's writings, often in aphoristic form, have been influential on modern art, philosophy, and psychology. Freud, for example, was amazed by Nietzsche's insights. Examples of Nietzsche's aphorism's on love abound in his *Beyond Good and Evil*: Whoever first expressed love of humankind "for God's sake . . . let him for all time be holy and respected, as the man who has so far flown highest and gone astray in the finest fashion!" Christianity makes "a *sublime abortion* of man." "Not their love of humanity, but the impotence of their love, prevents the Christians of today [from] burning us." "Even concubinage has been corrupted – by marriage." "In revenge and in love woman is more barbarous than man." "Christianity gave Eros poison to drink; he did not die of it, certainly, but degenerated to Vice." "One loves ultimately one's desires, not the thing desired." Nietzsche's misogynism, while not unique to his time, also expressed his aphoristic skills. In *Thus Spake Zarathustra*, Nietzsche wrote: "Everything in woman is a riddle, and everything in woman hath one solution – it is called pregnancy." Peter Gay notes that "To be a woman and to be Christian is, for Nietzsche, practically the same thing. Woman, physically feeble, needs a 'religion of weakness, which she glorifies as divine,' in order to be 'weak, to love, to be humble'. . . . " Nygren notes: "Nietzsche quite rightly saw that Christian love means the transvaluation of those values of antiquity which he himself valued most highly; . . . "

"Love" had a novelistic bonanza in the nineteenth century when, as Peter Gay notes, "love dominated the fiction of civilized countries." One of these writers is Stendhal (Marie-Henri Beyle, 1783–1842). After working in the French administration and participating in Napoleon's Russian campaign, Stendhal settled in Italy. While he gained a reputation as a womanizer, his empathy toward women and their emancipation is evident in his novels, the most famous of which are *The Red and the Black* and *The Charterhouse of Parma*. Unique among the Romantics, however, he also wrote an analysis of "the malady called Love," *De l'Amour* (*On Love*). He attributed the boredom and emptiness of bourgeois marriages to pervasive male chauvinism that wants women to be empty-headed "Barbie dolls" while at the same time dutifully maintaining the household. Stendhal argued love cannot exist without mutual esteem, and that means the liberation of women from a culturally imposed domesticity and for education and development of imagination. A cultured imagination, he argued, is essential to love.

Stendhal invented the term "crystallization" for the birth and growth of love. Love is like a bare branch thrown into a salt mine that with time becomes covered with glittering crystals. Love endows the beloved with crystals of beauty and desirability as the salt did with the bare branch. The process in relation to the one who becomes loved occurs in steps of admiration, acknowledgment of response, hope of gaining the other's love, and delight in overrating the beauty and merit of the beloved. Love relativizes beauty; the lover's eye sees beyond faults and ennobles them. So he wrote that "Love is the only passion that mints the coin to pay its own expenses." Thus "doubt is the natural outcome of crystallization." Is this an echo of Schopenhauer's view that love is delusional and illusional? Ortega y Gasset thinks that "the theory of 'crystallization' is pessimistic. It tries to show that what we consider normal functions of our spirit are nothing more than special cases of abnormality." "[T]he external object for which we live [is] a mere projection of the individual." He continues: "with the theory of 'crystallization' . . . a man loves only what is lovable, what is worthy of being loved." Here again, we see a variation on the old theme of eros. Brümmer says that for Stendhal love dies without continual fantasy to keep it alive. "In this sense Stendhal's lover is in fact a solipsist. His love is not directed to a real person, but only to the products of his own fantasy. His love creates its own object."

We began with the oft-noted observation that the concept of love in Western culture has roots in both Greco-Roman culture and biblical culture. In our whirlwind tour through the ages we have seen the main expressions – eros and agape – as rivals, opponents, and, at times, siblings. We close our kaleidoscope of history with two major modern representatives of these views: Anders Nygren and Paul Tillich.

The seminal modern study of the concept of love is Anders Nygren's *Agape and Eros*. Nygren (1890–1978), student and then Professor of Theology at Lund University in Sweden, became the bishop of Lund in 1948 and was ecumenically active as President of the Lutheran World Federation and in the Faith and Order department of the World Council of Churches. *Agape and Eros*, written originally in Swedish in two parts, "A Study in the Christian Idea of Love" (1930) and "The History of the Christian Idea of Love" (1936), appeared nearly immediately in German and English translations. McGinn refers to this book as "[t]he most famous modern investigation of the relations of agape and eros in the history of Christian thought...." Likewise, Outka terms Nygren's book "[t]he most influential formulation of the content of God's grace or agape (used interchangeably in this case), especially for Protestants...." Others, especially Roman Catholic scholars such as Burnaby and D'Arcy, are critical of Nygren's disjunction of eros and agape and see it as the source of Nygren's mistaken interpretations of various historical figures, especially Augustine and Thomas. Hampson highlights the significance of Nygren's study with an entire chapter titled "Nygren's Detractors." Attestations to the influence, pro and con, of Nygren's study are legion for his work shaped the contemporary discussion of love beyond the field of religious studies while also providing the basic vocabulary for the discussion. A case in point is Pope Benedict XVI's encyclical, *Deus Caritas Est* (2005; Ratzinger, now Benedict XVI, contributed the entry on the history of the theology of love to the 1961 edition of the *Lexikon für Theologie und Kirche*), the first part of which discusses the vocabulary of eros and agape. It would take us too far afield into ecumenics to discuss thoroughly the Pope's encyclical. What is interesting in relation to our survey is Benedict's emphasis upon the unity of eros and agape, his positive view of ancient ladder imagery depicting eros as ascent in ecstasy toward God, and his bold use of the medieval fascination with the rare naming of God as Eros by the fifth-century Neoplatonist, Dionysius the Pseudo-Areopagite; in short, the Augustinian synthesis of eros and agape and the Thomistic nature–grace continuity are alive and well in Benedict's encyclical. Thus Benedict's criticism of Nygren's study, without naming him, is not surprising. Nor is it a surprise to read the specific condemnations of Nygren's work in the numerous Roman Catholic commentaries on the encyclical. Hampson argues that such Catholic criticisms and condemnations arise from a basic misunderstanding of Nygren's work due to the tendency to equate eros with creation and agape with redemption, i.e., the schema of nature and grace in which grace completes nature. Hampson's point is that this misunderstanding reflects different thought structures between Catholic and Protestant theologies.

Agape and Eros is the fruit of Nygren's method of analysis, motif research. By use of this method, Nygren intended to set forth and to clarify the distinctive character of the Christian concept of love and its role in the history of Christianity. A premise of motif research is that similar concepts may have different or even antithetical meanings dependent upon their basic presuppositions. We sometimes experience this in conversations that can veer off in a direction that may surprise us when our conversation partner understands a word we use in a quite different sense than we intended. In his "Translator's Preface" to *Agape and Eros*, Philip Watson explains that the motif concealed behind similar or identical terms and expressions is discovered as the answer that is supplied by any given system to a fundamental question. Religion is generally defined as fellowship with the eternal, with God. Therefore, the question that explicates the fundamental motif of any religious system is: "How is fellowship with God conceived; how is it supposed to be realized; in what does it consist? The answer to this question reveals the fundamental motif of the religion under discussion."

According to this method, the fundamental motif in Christianity is love, defined as agape. But, Nygren argues, the agape motif in Christianity has not gone uncontested; it has had to struggle constantly against the non-Christian motif of eros. It is critical to understand that "eros" here is not equivalent to "creation," "nature," "libido," or to "erotic" in the sense of sexuality. Rather, eros in Nygren's study is the Hellenistic philosophical and theological effort to acquire God, to achieve salvation. Echoing the older Protestant Liberal view of the Hellenization of the Gospel, Nygren argues that Western theology synthesized the self-giving love of the Christian revelation (agape) with the aspiring, acquisitive love (eros) of Greco-Roman philosophy and religion. According to Nygren, this synthesis has distorted both types of love because agape and eros are diametrically opposed loves. Agape is primarily God's love, even when expressed by humans. Agape is a descending love, from God to humankind. Agape is completely unselfish; it is sacrificial giving. Agape loves the other and thereby creates value in the other. Eros, on the other hand, is acquisitive desire; it is the ascending movement of human attempts to reach God (however perceived). Eros is egocentric and is the highest form of self-assertion. It is primarily an acquisitive desire that loves its object for the value it recognizes in it. The opposition between agape and eros may be expressed with the theological epigram that salvation is received not achieved. In Western Christian history, the synthesis of eros with agape has been graphically expressed in the image of the divinely provided ladder to heaven by which humankind climbs toward God.

The criticisms of Nygren's argument that agape and eros are two diametrically opposed loves basically make two points. One is that while his diagrammatic approach is helpful in clarifying motifs present in the conception of love as seen in the history of Christian thought, the clarification is jeopardized by the danger of misinterpretation inherent in over-systematization. The other point is that Nygren ends his study of the history of the Christian idea of love with Martin Luther who, Nygren claims, destroyed the synthesis of eros and agape and restored a purely theocentric relationship to God. Luther appears as the capstone to Nygren's thesis of agape and eros. Luther takes *the* normative position on Christian love. According to Nygren, Luther's "Copernican revolution" on the subject of love definitively settles the issue between eros and agape. Just as Copernicus shifted the Western understanding of the world from geocentric to heliocentric, so Luther shifted the understanding of religion from anthropocentric to theocentric, from eros to agape, from love to faith. Günther and Link in their article on love in the New Testament make a similar point: "*agape* [is] very close to concepts like *pistis*, – faith, *dikaiosyne*, – righteousness and, *charis* – grace, which all have a single point of origin in God alone." In his attack on egoistic or anthropocentric religion, Nygren shared the orientation of the Continental dialectical theologians such as Karl Barth who saw in the Enlightenment and then the Liberal theology prior to World War I the twin problems of the humanization of God and the divinization of humankind so famously expressed by Ludwig Feuerbach in the assertions that love is God, and theology is anthropology.

It is often argued that Nygren's method of motif research is reductionist and does not do justice to the historical material. It is not surprising that Roman Catholic scholars would respond to Nygren by emphasizing that his one-sided emphasis upon agape to the exclusion of eros leaves no place for any properly human response to God. The Jesuit scholar M. C. D'Arcy argues that a love that excludes the self is no love at all, and that the consequence of Nygren's position is to eliminate human love altogether. That is, the stress upon agape and the removal of all self-love eliminates the person as person. Hampson retorts that D'Arcy's book is "about many things and clarity is not its greatest asset! D'Arcy is a neo-Platonist or Augustinian, a Thomist, and also very much a Jesuit. It will not surprise us by now that he thoroughly misreads Nygren."

Nygren's rigorous opposition of agape and eros is both affirmed and modified by another Protestant theologian, Karl Barth (1886–1968). Barth thinks Nygren's eyes "are oversharpened by the controversial theology of Sweden." And while Barth himself maintains the distinction between agape and eros, he questions whether this opposition can ever be fully overcome in history. Furthermore, agape is grounded in God's love for humankind, thus since its existence is not dependent upon its antithesis to eros, it does not need to insist upon this antithesis. "[E]ven erotic man must and will be affirmed in and with the love which is from God – Christian love."

Other critiques of Nygren's book focus on his interpretation of particular historical figures. Classicists and Plato scholars have been particularly offended. Osborne's work, for example, is directed against Nygren's contribution to "a popular prejudice against Plato, and against the 'Platonic love' that is essential to true philosophy for Plato." Nygren responded to many of his critics by pointing out he was not making a value judgment about ideas or persons but rather positing an ideal typology to clarify thinking about the concept of love. In his "Intellectual Autobiography" Nygren states: "The task of scientific scholarship is to describe not to evaluate. Again and again in my work it is emphasized that the terms agape and eros are not used as value judgements, but purely and exclusively as descriptions." Nygren makes the same point in his "Reply to Interpreters and Critics."

The Protestant theologian Paul Tillich (1886–1965) called for a more inclusive view of love and stressed the unity of love, power, and justice. In *Love, Power, and Justice* Tillich argued that distinctions about the nature of love as types rather than qualities are misleading. This error is avoided, Tillich claimed, by relating love to being. "The ontology of love leads to the basic assertion that love is one." Tillich's point, echoing Plato as well as Paul, is that throughout human history there runs the experience of estrangement, of separation. "Love is the drive towards the unity of the separated. Reunion presupposes separation of that which belongs essentially together. . . . Therefore love cannot be described as the union of the strange but as the reunion of the estranged. Estrangement presupposes original oneness. Love manifests its greatest power there where it overcomes the greatest separation. And the greatest separation is the separation of self from self." In terms of self-love, a person "can love himself in terms of self-acceptance only if he is certain that he is accepted." Thus within the unity of love there is room for self-love, and self-love has a valid place within the Christian conception of love. "Without the desire of man to be reunited with his origin, the love towards God becomes a meaningless word." The parallels of Tillich's views with those of Erich Fromm's *The Art of Loving* are striking.

Born and educated in Germany, Tillich was ordained a parish pastor and his early experience in a working class parish in Berlin was an impetus to his later advocacy of religious socialism. With the outbreak of World War I, he volunteered as a field chaplain and experienced the horrors of that war in a variety of places including Verdun. His academic dissertations on Shelling and Schleiermacher reflected his interest in the Romantic movement, and prepared him for an academic career in philosophy and theology. However his early criticism of National Socialism and Hitler barred Tillich from teaching in Germany, and in 1933 he accepted the invitation to teach at Union Theological Seminary in New York City (1933–1955). He then had successive positions at Harvard Divinity School (1955–1962) and the University of Chicago Divinity School (1962 –1965). From the outset, he understood himself to be a theologian of the boundaries where philosophy and theology, religion and culture, faith and politics, and – in terms of our interest – eros and agape met and interacted.

In *Biblical Religion and the Search for Ultimate Reality* Tillich asserted: "The God of Abraham, Isaac, and Jacob and the God of the philosophers is the same God." The prophet of agape is not in absolute opposition to the philosopher in quest of being itself.

> Where *agape* (the biblical term for "love") is put into an absolute contrast to *eros* (the Platonic term for "love"), no positive relation of biblical religion to ontology is seen. But this presupposes a distortion of the meaning both of *agape* and of *eros*. . . . *Eros* drives the soul through all levels of reality to ultimate reality, to truth itself, which is the good itself. . . . Certainly *agape* adds a decisive element to the ancient idea of love, but it does not deny the drive for cognitive union with ultimate reality. *Agape* reaches down to the lowest, forgiving its estrangement and reuniting it with the highest. But *agape* does not contradict the desire for the highest; and a part of this desire is cognitive *eros*.

Philosophical discussions of ontology, of being united with Being, may provide profound insights into love; they can also

create headaches and stomachaches. Tillich himself acknow-
ledged that his sermons were more easily digested than his
philosophical theology. Thus we turn to Tillich's sermons as
the conclusion to his perspective.

Tillich based his sermon "The Power of Love" on the texts
concerning the sheep and the goats at the Last Judgment
(Matt. 25:31–40) and the Johannine statement that the person
"who abides in love abides in God, and God abides in him"
(1 John 4:16).

> God and love are not two realities; they are one. . . . Therefore,
> he who professes devotion to God *may* abide in God if he abides
> in love, or he may not abide in God if he does not abide in love.
> And he who does not speak of God may abide in Him if he is
> abiding in love. And since the manifestation of God as love
> is His manifestation in Jesus the Christ, Jesus can say that
> many of those who do not know Him, belong to Him, and
> that many of those who confess their allegiance to Him do not
> belong to Him. The criterion, the only ultimate criterion, is love.

Tillich then tells the story of Elsa Brandström, daughter of the
Swedish ambassador to Russia during World War I, who,
moved by seeing the German prisoners of war, became a nurse
in prison camps. She witnessed and experienced "unspeakable
horrors" and "brutality" while serving the sick, despairing,
prisoners. After the war she initiated work for the orphans
of German and Russian prisoners of war; and when forced
out of Germany by the Nazis she moved to America to assist
European refugees. Tillich, who knew her for some ten years,
said:

> We never had a theological conversation. It was unnecessary.
> She made God transparent in every moment. For God, who is
> love, was abiding in her and she in Him. She aroused the love of
> millions toward herself and towards that for which she was

transparent – the God who is love.... It is a rare gift to meet a human being in whom love – and this means God – is so overwhelmingly manifest. It undercuts theological arrogance as well as pious isolation. It is more than justice and it is greater than faith and hope. It is the presence of God Himself. For God is love. And in every moment of genuine love we are dwelling in God and God in us.

We began with allusions to the relationship of Eros and Thanatos, and we have seen the dark desire for death along our way, for example with Tristan and Isolde. The present time all too often seems to be equally enthralled by such life denial. We seem to have fallen in love with death. The monuments of the present are death (economic exploitation is perhaps a greater weapon of mass destruction than war) not love. Tillich personally knew the terrors of war – at 28 he wrote his father from the trenches : "Hell rages around us. It's unimaginable." Later in *Theology of Culture* he referred to Picasso's painting of the bombing of Guernica as an outstanding example of the artistic expression of "man's finitude, his subjection to death, but above all, his estrangement from his true being and his bondage to demonic forces – forces of self-destruction." Tillich himself knew these forces firsthand, yet he affirmed that "love is stronger than death." In his sermon with that title, based on 1 John 3:14 ("He who does not love remains in death."), he wrote:

> But who can look at this picture [of destruction and death]? Only he who can look at another picture and beyond it – the picture of Love. For love is stronger than death. Every death means parting, separation, isolation, opposition and not participation.... Our souls become poor and disintegrate insofar as we want to be alone, insofar as we bemoan our misfortunes, nurse our despair and enjoy our bitterness, and yet turn coldly away from the physical and spiritual needs of others. Love

overcomes separation and creates participation in which there is more than that which the individuals involved can bring to it. Love is the infinite which is given to the finite.

It is love, human and divine, which overcomes death in nations and generations and in all the horror of our time. Help has become almost impossible in the face of the monstrous powers which we are all experiencing. Death is given power over everything finite, especially in our period of history. But death is given no power over love. Love is stronger. It creates something new out of the destruction caused by death; it bears everything and overcomes everything. . . . It is omnipresent and here and there, in the smallest and most hidden ways as in the greatest and most visible ones, it rescues life from death. It rescues each of us, for love is stronger than death.

Conclusion

Concluding Unscientific Postscript

There is no conclusion to the history of love. On the other hand, after wading through just a few of the innumerable stories and philosophical and theological reflections on love, it may be possible to provide a perspective under the rubric of Kierkegaard's suggestive phrase: "Concluding Unscientific Postscript."

Throughout the above pell-mell rush through a few millennia of views on love I have used the terms "eros" and "agape" as conceptual entrées to sort through the fundamental Hellenistic and biblical sources informing Western reflections. Now I have much greater appreciation of C. S. Lewis's reflection in the "Introduction" to his *The Four Loves*: "I was looking forward to writing some easy panegyrics of the first sort of love [God's "Gift-love"] and disparagements of the second [Plato's "Need-love"]. And much of what I was going to say still seems to me to be true." But, Lewis continues, "I cannot now deny the name *love* to Need-love. Every time I have tried to think the thing out alone those lines I have ended in puzzles and contradictions. The reality is more complicated than I supposed."

"The reality is more complicated than I supposed." It occurs to me now that another paradigm may also serve as a clue to the relationship of need and gift to love. Perhaps we could think of the interaction of the twin sources of our culture's views on love in terms of a tale of two banquets. The two banquets are Plato's *Symposium* and the biblical accounts of the Messianic banquet including Jesus's last supper. The former celebrates love as the means for transcendence, for ascent from this world of illusion, disappointment, and death to the world of ideas, the "real" world of beauty and the good. The consequent orientation to life is eudaemonism – the drive for happiness, for well-being. The latter celebrates love as imminent relationships in this world in the midst of failure and death. In Isaiah, God's "everlasting covenant," his "steadfast, sure love for David" is the basis for inviting the poor to a joyful banquet. "Ho, everyone who thirsts, come to the waters; and you that have no money, come, buy and eat! Come, buy wine and milk without money and without price" (Isa. 55:1–3). The banquet is inclusive. "The Lord of hosts will make for all peoples a feast of rich food, a feast of well-aged wines, of rich food filled with marrow, of well-aged wines strained clear" (Isa. 25:6). The examples can be multiplied from the manna of the Exodus to the oil and bread of Elisha to the feedings of the multitudes in the New Testament. The theme of food runs throughout the Gospel of Luke. Here too the banquet is inclusive. "The Son of Man has come eating and drinking" and is called "a glutton and drunkard, a friend of tax collectors and sinners!" (Luke 7:34). God is the host of the banquet from the Passover celebration to the Last Supper symbolized in the words "for you" and "for many." The Last Supper banquet is both the echo of Israel's Passover celebration of deliverance from bondage and the conclusion to the "first of his [Jesus's] signs," the changing of water into wine – some 180 gallons! – at the wedding in Cana (John 2:1–11). The consequent orientation to life is eucharistia – thanksgiving – that extends to and includes others.

More often than not, artists are able vividly to portray and evoke what historians and theologians pile up words to express and attempt to explain. Nowhere, I think, has the banquet image been more beautifully portrayed than in Isak Dinesen's (Karen Blixen, 1885–1962) short story "Babette's Feast" and its much discussed film version. Babette, a famous Parisian chef, in flight for her life from a revolt that has killed her husband and son, is almost literally washed up upon a small Scandinavian village of Lutheran Pietists. Taken in by the daughters of the deceased pastor, Martine and Philippa (named for the Reformers Martin Luther and Philipp Melanchthon), Babette becomes their maid. After 14 years in the community of aging Pietists, the faithful remnant of the pastor's ministry, Babette learns she has won 10,000 francs in the French lottery. When the daughters contemplate commemorating the 100th anniversary of their father's birth, Babette convinces them to allow her to prepare a celebration dinner. Unbeknownst to the sisters, Babette spends all her money to prepare one of her famous meals from her past life as chef at the Café Anglais in Paris, meals described as "a kind of love affair . . . in which one no longer distinguishes between bodily and spiritual appetite or satiety!" Dinesen invokes one biblical banquet image after another as she tells this story: manna, the wedding at Cana, exotic wines with every course, the 12 guests, and the *pièce de résistance* of the meal – *cailles en sarcophage* (quails in pastry shells) – that evokes both the manna of the Exodus and Jesus's three days in the tomb. The participants, each burdened with the regrets and sins accumulated through long lives, are transformed by the gratuitous presence of such abundance of food, wine, and love. Toward the end of the banquet, an outsider to the small group, General Loewenhielm, who in his youth had fallen in love with Martine but had left her for a successful worldly career rose and gave a speech:

> "Man, my friends," said General Loewenhielm, "is frail and foolish. We have all of us been told that grace is to be found in the universe. But in our human foolishness and short-sightedness we imagine divine grace to be finite. For this reason we tremble.... But the moment comes when our eyes are opened, and we see and realize that grace is infinite. Grace, my friends, demands nothing from us but that we shall await it with confidence and acknowledge it in gratitude. Grace brothers makes no conditions and singles out none of us in particular; grace takes us all to its bosom and proclaims general amnesty. See! that which we have chosen is given us, and that which we have refused is, also and at the same time, granted us. Ay, that which we have rejected is poured upon us abundantly. For mercy and truth have met together, and righteousness and bliss have kissed one another!"

The dialogues and conflicts over love in Western culture are reflected in General Loewenhielm's speech. Is it not "perhaps too rarely considered," asks Josef Pieper, "that even the very first stirrings of love contain an element of gratitude? But gratitude is a reply; it is knowing that one has been referred to something prior, in this case to a larger frame of universal reference...."

Bibliography

The following bibliography is limited to studies consulted and/or cited. Each entry itself contains extensive bibliography. For overviews of the concept of love in Eastern religions, Judaism, and Islam including extensive bibliographies see the entries "Liebe" in *Theologische Realenzyklopädie*, Vol. 21 (Berlin, New York: Walter de Gruyter, 1991), 122–8, 133–8 and *Religion in Geschichte und Gegenwart*, Vol. 5 (Tübingen: Mohr Siebeck, 2002), 335–6, 348–9, 356–9.

Abelard, Peter, *The Story of My Misfortunes*, Henry Adams Bellows, trans., New York: The Macmillan Company, 1972.

Allen, Peter L., *The Art of Love. Amatory Fiction from Ovid to the Romance of the Rose*, Philadelphia: University of Pennsylvania Press, 1992.

Aquinas, Thomas, *On Charity*, Lottie H. Kendzierski, trans., Milwaukee: Marquette University Press, 1984.

Arendt, Hannah, *Love and Saint Augustine* (1929), edited and with an Interpretative Essay by Joanna Vecchiarelli Scott and Judith Chelius Stark, Chicago: University of Chicago Press, 1996.

Aristotle, *Metaphysics*, Richard Hope, trans., Ann Arbor: University of Michigan Press, 1960.

—— *Nicomachean Ethics*, Martin Oswald, trans., The Library of Liberal Arts, Indianapolis/New York: Bobbs-Merrill, 1962.

Armstrong, A. H., "Platonic Eros and Christian Agape," *Downside Review* 79 (1961), 105–21. Repr. in *idem, Plotinian and Christian Studies*, London: Variorum Reprints, 1979.

Armstrong, Regis J., *St. Francis of Assisi. Writings for a Gospel Life*, New York: Crossroad, 1994.

—— J. A. Wayne Hellmann, and William J. Short, eds. *Francis of Assisi: Early Documents*, Vol. 1: *The Saint*, New York: New City Press, 1999.

Arndt, Johann, *Sechs Bücher vom wahren Christenthum, nebst dessen Paradies-Gärtlein*, Stuttgart: Steinkopf, nd.

Astell, Ann W., *The Song of Songs in the Middle Ages*, Ithaca & London: Cornell University Press, 1990.

Augenstein, Jörg, *Das Liebesgebot im Johannesevangelium und in den Johannisbriefen*, Stuttgart: Kohlhammer, 1993.

Augustine, Aurelius, *Basic Writings of Saint Augustine*, Whitney J. Oates, ed., 2 vols., New York: Random House, 1948.

Baron, Robert, *Thomas Aquinas: Spiritual Master*, New York: Crossroad, 1996.

Barr, James, "Words for Love in Biblical Greek" in L. D. Hurst and N. T. Wright, eds., *The Glory of Christ in the New Testament. Studies in Christology. In Memory of George Bradford Caird*, Oxford: Clarendon Press, 1987, 3–18.

Barth, Karl, *Church Dogmatics*, IV/2, section 68: "The Holy Spirit and Christian Love," G. W. Bromily and T. F. Torrance, trans., Edinburgh: T. & T. Clark, 1958.

—— *Evangelical Theology: An Introduction*, Grover Foley, trans., New York: Holt, Rinehart and Winston, 1963.

—— *Protestant Theology in the Nineteenth Century*, Valley Forge: Judson Press, 1973.

Baumer, Franklin L., *Modern European Thought. Continuity and Change in Ideas, 1600–1950*, New York: Macmillan, 1977.

Benedict XVI, *Deus Caritas Est*, Vatican City: Libreria Editrice Vaticana, 2006.

Benton, John F., "Clio and Venus: An Historical View of Medieval Love" in F. X. Newman, ed., *The Meaning of Courtly Love*, Albany: State University of New York Press, 1968, 19–42.

Berardino, Angelo di, "Monnica" in Fitzgerald, ed., *Augustine through the Ages*, 570–71.

Bernard of Clairvaux, *On the Song of Songs*, 4 vols., Kilian Walsh, trans., Kalamazoo: Cistercian Publications, 1971–1980.

—— *On Loving God*, with an Analytical Commentary by Emero Stiegman, Kalamazoo: Cistercian Publications, 1995.

Beyreuther, Erich, *Geschichte der Diakonie und Inneren Mission in der Neuzeit*, Berlin: Christlicher Zeitschriftenverlag, 1983.

Bielecki, Tessa, ed., *Teresa of Avila. Mystical Writings*, New York: Crossroad, 1994.

Boase, R., *The Origin and Meaning of Courtly Love*, Manchester: Manchester University Press, 1977.

Boccaccio, Giovanni, *The Decameron*, Frances Winwar, trans., New York: Random House, 1955.

Bolkestein, Hendrik, *Wohltätigkeit und Armenpflege im vorchristlichen Altertum*, 1939; repr. New York: Arno Press, 1979.

Bowery, Anne-Marie, "Plotinus, *The Enneads*" in Fitzgerald, ed., *Augustine through the Ages*, 654–57.

Brady, Bernard V., *Christian Love. How Christians through the Ages Have Understood Love*, Washington, DC: Georgetown University Press, 2003.

Brechkten, Josef, *Augustinus Doctor Caritatis. Sein Liebesbegriff im Widerspruch von Eigennutz und selbstloser Güte im Rahmen der antiken Glückseligkeits-Ethik*, Meisenheim am Glan: Anton Hain, 1975.

Brown, Peter, *The Body and Society. Men, Women, and Sexual Renunciation in Early Christianity*, New York: Columbia University Press, 1988.

Brown, Raymond E., Joseph A. Fitzmyer, and Roland E. Murphy, eds., *The New Jerome Biblical Commentary*, Englewood Cliffs: Prentice Hall, 1990.

Brümmer, Vincent, *The Model of Love: A Study in Philosophical Theology*, Cambridge: Cambridge University Press, 1993.

Brunn, Emilie Zum and Georgette Epiney-Burgard, *Women Mystics in Medieval Europe*, Sheila Hughes, trans., New York: Paragon House, 1989.

Bucer, Martin, *Instruction in Christian Love*, Paul T. Fuhrmann, trans., Richmond: John Knox Press, 1952.

Burge, James, *Heloise and Abelard. A New Biography*, New York: HarperSanFrancisco, 2003.

Burnaby, John, "Amor in St. Augustine" in C. W. Kegley, *The Philosophy and Theology of Anders Nygren*, 174–86.

—— *Amor Dei. A Study of the Religion of St. Augustine*, London, 1938; Norwich: The Canterbury Press, 1991.

Camille, Michael, *The Medieval Art of Love, Objects and Subjects of Desire*, New York: Abrams, 1998.

Capellanus, Andreas, *The Art of Courtly Love*, John Jay Parry, trans., New York: W. W. Norton with Columbia University Press, 1969.

Cheyette, Fredric L., *Ermengard of Narbonne and the World of the Troubadours*, Ithaca: Cornell University Press, 2001.

Chrétien de Troyes, *Arthurian Romances*, W. W. Comfort, trans. (1914), London and Melbourne: Dent, 1984.

Clack, Beverley, *Sex and Death: A Reappraisal of Human Mortality*, Cambridge: Polity Press, 2002.

Clanchy, M. T., *Abelard. A Medieval Life*, Oxford: Blackwell, 1997.

Clark, Elizabeth, ed., *St. Augustine on Marriage and Sexuality*, Washington, DC: The Catholic University of America Press, 1996.

Classen, Albrecht, "Hadewijch als erotische Liebesdichterin," *Studies in Spirituality*, 12 (2002), 23–42.

Clements, Keith W., ed., *Friedrich Schleiermacher. Pioneer of Modern Theology*, Minneapolis: Fortress Press, 1991.

Countryman, L. Wm., *The Rich Christian in the Church of the Early Empire*. New York/Toronto: The Edwin Mellen Press, 1980.

Crowner, David and Gerald Christianson, eds. and trans., *The Spirituality of the German Awakening*, New York: Paulist Press, 2003.

Dante, *The Divine Comedy*, John Ciardi, trans., New York/ London: Norton, 1970.

D'Arcy, M. C., *The Mind and Heart of Love. A Study in Eros and Agape*, rev. edn., New York: Meridion Books, 1960.

Dideberg, Dany, *S. Augustin et la première Epitre de S. Jean. Une théologie de l'agapè*, Paris: Éditions Beauchesne, 1975.

Dinesen, Isak, "Babette's Feast" in *idem, Anecdotes of Destiny and Ehrengard*, New York: 1993, 19–59.

Dinzelbacher, Peter, "Über die Entdeckung der Liebe im Hochmittelalter," *Saeculum* 32 (1981), 185–208.

—— "Liebe" in *Lexikon des Mittelalters*, Vol. 5, Robert Auty, gen. ed., Munich/Zurich: Artemis, 1991, Columns 1965–1968.

Elliot, Mark W., *The Song of Songs and Christology in the Early Church 381–451*, Tübingen: Mohr Siebeck, 2000.

Els, P. J. J. S., "Love" in Willam A. VanGemeren, General Editor, *The New International Dictionary of Old Testament Theology and Exegesis*, Grand Rapids: Zondervan, 1997, 1: 277–99.

Eusebius, *The History of the Church from Christ to Constantine*, G. A. Williamson, trans., Harmondsworth: Penguin Books, 1965, repr. 1981.

Evans, G. R., *The Mind of St. Bernard of Clairvaux*, Oxford: Clarendon Press, 1983.

—— *Bernard of Clairvaux*, New York: Oxford University Press, 2000.

—— ed., *The Medieval Theologians. An Introduction to Theology in the Medieval Period*, Oxford: Blackwell, 2001.

Feuerbach, Ludwig, *The Essence of Christianity*, George Eliot, trans., New York: Harper, 1957.

Ficino, Marsilio, *Commentary on Plato's* Symposium *on Love*, Sears Jayne, trans., Dallas: Spring Publications, 1985.

Fiorenza, Francis Schüssler, "Marriage" in *idem* and John P. Galvin, eds., *Systematic Theology. Roman Catholic Perspectives*, 2 vols., Minneapolis: Fortress Press, 1991, Vol. 1, 307–46.

Fitzgerald, Allen D., ed., *Augustine through the Ages: An Encyclopedia*, Grand Rapids: W. B. Eerdmans, 1999.

Flacelière, Robert, *Love in Ancient Greece*, New York: Crown Publishers, 1962.

Fleteren, Frederick Van, "Ascent of the Soul" in Fitzgerald, ed., *Augustine through the Ages*, 63–7.

—— "Plato, Platonism" in Fitzgerald, ed., *Augustine through the Ages*, 651–4.

Forell, George W., *Faith Active in Love. An Investigation of the Principles Underlying Luther's Social Ethics*, Minneapolis: Augsburg, 1954.

Fromm, Erich, *The Art of Loving. An Inquiry into the Nature of Love*, New York: Harper & Row, 1956.

Furnish, Victor Paul, *The Love Command in the New Testament*, Nashville: Abingdon Press, 1972.

Gay, Peter, *The Bourgeois Experience. Victoria to Freud*, Vol. 2, *The Tender Passion*, New York: Oxford University Press, 1986.

Gennrich, F., *Troubadours, Trouvères, Minnesang and Meistergesang*, Cologne: Arno Volk Verlag, 1960.

Gerth, H. H. and C. Wright Mills, eds., *From Max Weber: Essays in Sociology*, New York: Oxford University Press, 1946, repr. 1967.

Gilson, Etienne, *The Mystical Theology of Saint Bernard*, A. H. C. Downes, trans., Kalamazoo: Cistercian Publications repr., 1990.

Gonzalez, Justo, *Faith and Wealth: A History of Early Christian Ideas on the Origin, Significance, and Use of Money*, San Francisco: Harper & Row, 1990.

Green, Ronald M., "Kant on Christian Love" in Edmund N. Santurri and William Werpehowski, eds., *The Love Commandments: Essays in Christian Ethics and Moral Philosophy*, Washington, DC: Georgetown University Press, 1992, 261–80.

Günther, W., H.-G. Link, and C. Brown, "Love" in Colin Brown, gen. ed., *The New International Dictionary of New Testament Theology*, Grand Rapids: Zondervan, 1986, 2:538–51.

Gurevich, Aaron, *The Origins of European Individualism*, Katherine Judelson, trans., Oxford: Blackwell, 1995.

Hamm, Berndt, *The Reformation of Faith in the Context of Late Medieval Theology and Piety*, Robert J. Bast, ed., Leiden: Brill, 2004.

Hampson, Daphne, *Christian Contradictions. The Structures of Lutheran and Catholic Thought*, Cambridge: Cambridge University Press, 2001.

Hanawalt, Emily Albu and C. Lindberg, eds., *Through the Eye of a Needle: Judeo-Christian Roots of Social Welfare*, Kirksville: Thomas Jefferson University Press, 1994.

Hands, A. R., *Charities and Social Aid in Greece and Rome*, Ithaca: Cornell University Press, 1968.

Harnack, Adolf von, *The Expansion of Christianity in the First Three Centuries*, 2 vols., James Moffatt, trans., London: Williams & Norgate/New York: Putnam's Sons, 1904.

Harrison, Carol, *Augustine. Christian Truth and Fractured Humanity*, Oxford: Oxford University Press, 2000.

Hawkins, Peter S., *Dante. A Brief History*, Oxford: Blackwell, 2006.

Heck, Christian, *L'Échelle Céleste dans L'Art du Moyen Âge. Une Histoire de la Quête du Ciel*, Paris: Flammarion, 1997.

Hesiod, *Theogony*, Norman O. Brown, trans., The Library of Liberal Arts, New York: Macmillan, 1986.

Hopkins, Andrea, *The Book of Courtly Love. The Passionate Code of the Troubadours*, San Francisco: HarperSanFrancisco, 1994.

Ide, Pascal, "La distinction entre *éros* et *agapè* dans *Deus caritas est* de Benoît XVI," *Nouvelle Revue Théologique* 128 (2006), 353–69.

Irwin, Alexander, *Eros Toward the World. Paul Tillich and the Theology of the Erotic*, Minneapolis: Fortress Press, 1991.

Jaeger, C. Stephen, *Ennobling Love. In Search of a Lost Sensibility*, Philadelphia: University of Pennsylvania Press, 1999.

Jenni, Ernst and Claus Westermann, eds. *Theological Lexicon of the Old Testament*, Mark Biddle, trans., Peabody: Hendrickson Publishers, 1997.

Johann Hinrich Wichern und das Rauhe Haus, Hamburg: Rauhes Haus, 1953.

Johannesson, R., "Caritas in Augustine and Medieval Theology" in C. W. Kegley, *The Philosophy and Theology of Anders Nygren*, 187–202.

Justin Martyr, "The First Apology of Justin" in *The Ante-Nicene Fathers*, Alexander Roberts and James Donaldson, eds., Grand Rapids: Eerdmans, 1953, Vol. 1.

Kegley, Charles W., ed., *The Philosophy and Theology of Anders Nygren*, Carbondale: Southern Illinois University Press, 1970.

Keller, Hildegard Elisabeth, *My Secret is Mine. Studies on Religion and Eros in the German Middle Ages*, Leuven: Peeters, 2000.

Kerr, Fergus, "Thomas Aquinas" in G. R. Evans, ed., *The Medieval Theologians*, 201–20.

Kidd, B. J., ed., *Documents Illustrative of the History of the Church*, 3 vols., New York: Macmillan, 1938.

King, Jr., Martin Luther, *Strength to Love*, Philadelphia: Fortress Press, 1981.

Kittel, Gerhard, ed., *Theological Dictionary of the New Testament*, Geoffrey W. Bromiley, trans. and ed., Grand Rapids: Eerdmans, 1964.

Kloft, Hans, ed., *Sozialmassnahmen und Fürsorge. Zur Eigenart Antiker Sozialpolitik*, Horn: Berger, 1988.

Kratz, Reinhardt and Hermann Spieckermann, eds., *Liebe und Gebot. Studien zum Deuteronomium*, Göttingen: Vandenhoeck & Ruprecht, 2000.

Kudlien, Fridolf, "'Krankensicherung' in der Griechischen-Römischen Antike" in Kloft, *Sozialmassnahmen*, 75–102.

Kuhn, Helmut, *"Liebe"Geschichte eines Begriffs*, Munich: Kösel Verlag, 1975.

—— "Liebe" in Joachim Ritter and Karlfried Gründer, eds., *Historisches Wörterbuch der Philosophie*, Vol. 5, Basel/Stuttgart: Schwabe, 1980, 290–318.

Lattke, Michael, *Einheit im Wort. Die spezifische Bedeutung von ἀγάπη, ἀγαπαν und φιλειν im Johannesevangelium*, Munich: Kösel-Verlag, 1975.

Lazar, Moshe and Norris J. Lacy, eds., *Poetics of Love in the Middle Ages: Texts and Contexts*, Fairfax, VA: George Mason University Press, 1989.

Leibbrand, Annemarie and Werner, *Formen des Eros. Kultur- und Geistesgeschichte der Liebe*, 2 vols., Freiburg/Munich: Karl Alber Verlag, 1972.

Lewis, C. S., *The Four Loves*, New York: Harcourt Brace Jovanovich, 1960.

Lindberg, Carter, "Further Reflections on Agape and Eros," *Lutheran Quarterly* 15/4 (1963), 338–44.

—— *Beyond Charity. Reformation Initiatives for the Poor*, Minneapolis: Fortress Press, 1993.

—— "The Future of a Tradition: Luther and the Family" in Dean O. Wenthe, et al., eds., *All Theology is Christology. Essays in Honor of David P. Scaer*, Fort Wayne: Concordia Theological Seminary Press, 2000, 133–51.

—— "Luther's Struggle with Social-Ethical Issues" in McKim, 165–78.

—— "Luther on Poverty" in Wengert, 134–51.

—— ed., *The Pietist Theologians*, Oxford: Blackwell, 2005.

Little, Lester K., *Religious Poverty and the Profit Economy in Medieval Europe*, Ithaca: Cornell University Press, 1978.

—— "Religion, the Profit Economy, and Saint Francis" in Hanawalt and Lindberg, 147–63.

Livingston, James C., *Modern Christian Thought: The Enlightenment and the Nineteenth Century*, 2nd edn., Upper Saddle River: Prentice Hall, 1997.

Lorris, Guillaume de and Jean de Meun, *The Romance of the Rose*, Harry W. Robbins, trans.; ed. with Introduction by Charles W. Dunn, New York: Dutton, 1962.

Lovejoy, Arthur O., *The Great Chain of Being. A Study of the History of an Idea* (1936), New York: Harper & Row, 1960.

Luther, Martin, *Luther's Works*, Jaroslav Pelikan and Helmut T. Lehmann, eds., 55 vols., St. Louis: Concordia/Philadelphia: Fortress, 1955–86.

Mannermaa, Tuomo, "Zwei Arten der Liebe" in *idem, Der im Glauben Gegenwärtige Christus. Rechtfertigung und Vergottung zum Ökumenischen Dialog*, Hannover: Lutherisches Verlagshaus, 1989, 107–81.

Markale, Jean, *L'Amour Courtois ou le couple infernal*, Paris: Editions Imago, 1987; English trans., Jon Graham, *Courtly Love: The Path of Sexual Initiation*, Rochester, VT: Inner Traditions International, 2000.

Martin, June Hall, *"Love's Fools:" Aucassin, Troilus, Calisto and the Parody of the Courtly Lover*, London: Tamesis Books, 1972.

Marrou, Henri, *Saint Augustine and his Influence through the Ages*, New York/London: Harper Torchbooks/Longmans, 1957.

Mathys, Hans-Peter, *Liebe Deinen Nächsten Wie Dich Selbst. Untersuchungen Zum alttestamentlichen Gebot der Nächstenliebe (Lev. 19,18)*, Göttingen: Vandenhoeck & Ruprecht, 1986.

Matthias, Markus, "August Hermann Francke (1663–1727)" in Lindberg, ed., *The Pietist Theologians*, 100–14.

McCarthy, Conor, ed., *Love, Sex and Marriage in the Middle Ages. A Sourcebook*, London and New York: Routledge, 2004.

McGinn, Bernard, "God as Eros. Metaphysical Foundations of Christian Mysticism" in Bradley Nassif, ed., *New Perspectives on Historical Theology. Essays in Memory of John Meyendorff*, Grand Rapids: Eerdmans, 1996, 189–209.

—— *The Flowering of Mysticism. Men and Women in the New Mysticism – 1200–1350*, New York: Crossroad, 1998.

McGuire, Brian Patrick, "Love, Friendship and Sex in the Eleventh Century: The Experience of Anselm," *Studia Theologica* 28 (1974), 111–52.

—— *Brother and Lover: Aelred of Rievaulx*, New York: Crossroad, 1994.

McKim, Donald K., ed., *The Cambridge Companion to Martin Luther*, Cambridge: Cambridge University Press, 2003.

Meisinger, Hubert, *Liebesgebot und Altruismusforschung. Ein exegetischer Beitrag Zum Dialog zwischen Theologie und Naturwissenschaft*, Göttingen: Vandenhoeck & Ruprecht, 1996.

Metzger, Bruce M. and Michael D. Coogan, eds., *The Oxford Companion to the Bible*, New York: Oxford University Press, 1993.

Mews, Constant J., *The Lost Love Letters of Heloise and Abelard. Perceptions of Dialogue in Twelfth-Century France*, New York: St. Martin's Press, 1999.

Milbank, John, "The Future of Love. A Reading of Pope Benedict XVI's Encyclical *Deus Caritas Est*," *Communio. International Catholic Review* 33/3 (Fall 2006), 368–74.

Miles, Margaret, *The Image and Practice of Holiness*, London: SCM, 1988.

Milhaven, John Giles, *Hadewijch and Her Sisters. Other Ways of Loving and Knowing*, Albany: State University of New York Press, 1993.

Miller, Timothy S., *The Birth of the Hospital in the Byzantine Empire*, Baltimore: The Johns Hopkins University Press, 1985.

Mollat, Michel, *The Poor in the Middle Ages. An Essay in Social History*, Arthur Goldhammer, trans., New Haven and London: Yale University Press, 1986.

Morgan, Douglas N., *Love: Plato, the Bible and Freud*, Englewood Cliffs: Prentice-Hall, Inc., 1964.

Morris, Colin, *The Discovery of the Individual 1050–1200*, London: SPCK, 1972; Toronto: University of Toronto Press, Medieval Academy Reprints, 1987.

Most, Glenn W., "Six Remarks on Platonic Eros" in Shadi Bartsch and Thomas Bartscherer, eds., *Erotikon. Essays on Eros, Ancient and Modern*, Chicago: University of Chicago Press, 2005, 33–47.

Muller, Richard A., *Dictionary of Latin and Greek Theological Terms. Drawn Principally from Protestant Scholastic Theology*, Grand Rapids: Baker Books, 1985.

Nielsen, Lauge O., "Peter Abelard and Gilbert of Poitiers" in Evans, *The Medieval Theologians*, 102–28.

Nietzsche, Friedrich, *The Philosophy of Nietzsche*, New York: The Modern Library, Random House, 1954.

Nikolaus, Wolfgang, "Eros und Agape," *Zeitschrift für Evangelische Ethik* 30 (1986), 399–420.

Nock, A. D., *Conversion. The Old and the New in Religion from Alexander the Great to Augustine of Hippo*, Oxford: Oxford University Press, 1965.

Novalis. His Life, Thoughts, and Works, M. J. Hope, trans. and ed., Chicago: McClurg & Co., 1891.

Novalis. Hymns to the Night and Other Selected Writings, Charles E. Passage, trans., New York: The Liberal Arts Press, 1960.

Nussbaum, Martha C., *The Fragility of Goodness. Luck and Ethics in Greek Tragedy and Philosophy*, Cambridge: Cambridge University Press, 1986, repr. 1988.

—— "*Eros* and Ethical Norms: Philosophers Respond to a Cultural Dilemma" in Nussbaum and Sihvola, *The Sleep of Reason*, 55–94.

—— and Juha Sihvola, eds., *The Sleep of Reason. Erotic Experience and Sexual Ethics in Ancient Rome and Greece*, Chicago: University of Chicago Press, 2002.

Nygren, Anders, *Agape and Eros*, Philip S. Watson, trans., Philadelphia: The Westminster Press, 1953.

—— "Intellectual Autobiography" in Kegley, 3–29.

—— "Reply to Interpreters and Critics" in Kegley, 347–75.

Oakley, Francis, *The Medieval Experience. Foundations of Western Cultural Singularity*, New York: Scribners', 1974; Toronto: University of Toronto Press, Medieval Academy Reprints, 1988.

Oberman, Heiko A., *Luther. Man between God and the Devil*, Eileen Walliser-Schwarzbart, trans., New Haven: Yale University Press, 1989.

O'Donovan, Oliver, *The Problem of Self-love in St. Augustine*, New Haven: Yale University Press, 1980.

Ortega y Gasset, José, *On Love. Aspects of a Single Theme*, Toby Talbot, trans., New York: Greenwich Editions (Meridian Books), 1957.

Osborne, Catherine, *Eros Unveiled: Plato and the God of Love*, Oxford: Clarendon Press, 1994.

Outka, Gene, *Agape. An Ethical Analysis*, New Haven and London: Yale University Press, 1972.

Ozment, Steven, *Protestants. The Birth of a Revolution*, New York: Doubleday, 1992.

Paolucci, Henry, "Introduction" in *idem*, ed., *St. Augustine. The Enchiridion on Faith, Hope and Love*, South Bend: Gateway Editions, Ltd., 1961.

Parlette, David, *Selections from the Carmina Burana. A Verse Translation*, London: Penguin Books, 1986.

Pearsall, Derek, *Arthurian Romance: A Short Introduction*, Oxford: Blackwell, 2003.

Perkins, Pheme, *Love Commands in the New Testament*, New York: Paulist Press, 1982.

Peters, F. E., *Greek Philosophical Terms: A Historical Lexicon*, New York: New York University Press, 1967.

Petré, Hélène, *Caritas. Étude sur le Vocabulaire Latin de la Charité Chrétienne*, Louvain: Spicilegium Sacrum Lovaniense, 1948.

Pieper, Josef, *About Love*, Richard and Clara Winston, trans., Chicago: Franciscan Herald Press, 1974.

Piper, John, *"Love your Enemies." Jesus' Love Command in the Synoptic Gospels and in the Early Christian Paraenesis. A History of the Tradition and Interpretation of its Uses*, Cambridge: Cambridge University Press, 1979.

Plato, *Symposium*, Benjamin Jowett, trans., New York: Bobbs-Merrill, 1956.

Plutarch, *Selected Essays: On Love, The Family, and The Good Life*, Moses Hadas, trans., New York: A Mentor Book, 1957.

Power, Kim, "Concubine/Concubinage" in Fitzgerald, ed., *Augustine through the Ages*, 222–3.

Prieur, Jean-Marc, "L'Éthique sexuelle et conjugale des Chrétiens des premiers siécles et ses justifications," *Revue d'histoire et de philosophie religieuses* 82/3 (2002), 267–82.

Radice, Betty, ed. and trans., *The Letters of Abelard and Heloise*, London: Penguin Books, 1974.

Rauschenbusch, Walter, *Dare We Be Christians?* (1914), repr. Cleveland: Pilgrim Press, 1993.

Redeker, Martin, *Schleiermacher: Life and Thought*, John Wallhausser, trans., Philadelphia: Fortress Press, 1973.

Rist, John M., *Eros and Psyche: Studies in Plato, Plotinus, and Origin*, Toronto: University of Toronto Press, 1964.

—— *Platonism and its Christian Heritage*, London: Variorum Reprints, 1985.

—— *Augustine. Ancient thought Baptized*, Cambridge: Cambridge University Press, 1994.

Riquet, Michel, S.J., *Christian Charity in Action*, P. J. Hepburne-Scott, trans., New York: Hawthorne Books, 1961.

Robertson, D. B., *Love and Justice. Selections from the Shorter Writings of Reinhold Niebuhr*, Philadelphia: Westminster Press, 1957.

Robertson, D. W., Jr., "The Doctrine of Charity in Mediaeval Literary Gardens: A Topical Approach Through Symbolism and Allegory," *Speculum* 26 (1951), 24–49.

Robinson, David M. and Edward J. Fluck, *A Study of the Greek Love-Names Including a Discussion of Paederasty and a Prosopographia*, Baltimore: The Johns Hopkins Press, 1937.

Rossiaud, Jacques, *Medieval Prostitution*, Lydia G. Cochrane, trans., Oxford: Blackwell, 1988.

Rougemont, Denis de, *Love in the Western World*. Montgomery Belgion, trans. Rev. ed., Princeton: Princeton University Press, 1983.

Rowland, Ingrid D., "The Architecture of Love in Baroque Rome" in Bartsch and Bartscherer, eds., *Erotikon*, 144–60.

Rudolph, Conrad, *The "Things of Greater Importance." Bernard of Clairvaux's "Apologia" and the Medieval Attitude Toward Art*, Philadelphia: University of Pennsylvania Press, 1990.

Schindler, D. C., "The Redemption of Eros: Philosophical Reflections on Benedict XVI's First Encyclical," *Communio. International Catholic Review* 33/3 (Fall 2006), 375–99.

Schlegel, Friedrich, *Atheneum Fragments*, German History Documents. http://germanhistorydocs.ghi-dc.org/sub_document.

Schleiermacher, Friedrich, *On Religion. Speeches to its Cultured Despisers*, John Oman trans., New York: Harper & Row, 1958.

Schneider, Gerhard, "αγάπη, ης, ή" [agape] in Horst Balz and Gerhard Schneider, eds., *Exegetical Dictionary of the New Testament*, Grand Rapids: Eerdmans, 1990, Vol. 1, 8–12.

Scholz, Heinrich, *Eros und Caritas. Die platonische Liebe und die Liebe im Sinne des Christentums*, Halle, 1929.

Schöpf, A., "Liebe" in Joachim Ritter and Karlfried Gründer, eds., *Historisches Wörterbuch der Philosophie*, Vol. 5, Basel/Stuttgart: Schwabe, 1980, 318–28.

Schwarz, Reinhard, "Die Umformung des religiösen Prinzips der Gottesliebe in der frühen Reformation" in Bernd Moeller, ed., *Die frühe Reformation in Deutschland als Umbruch*, Gütersloh: Gütersloher Verl.-Haus, 1998, 128–48.

Shapiro, Norman R., trans., *The Comedy of Eros. Medieval French Guides to the Art Of Love*, Urbana: University of Illinois Press, 2nd edn., 1997.

Söding, Thomas, *Das Liebesgebot bei Paulus. Die Mahnung zur Agape im Rahmen der paulinischen Ethik*, Münster: Aschendorff, 1995.

Spener, Philip Jakob, *Pia Desideria*, Theodore G. Tappert, trans., Philadelphia: Fortress Press, 1964.

Spicq, Ceslas, *Agapè dans le NT*, 3 vols., 1958/59.

—— *Agape in the New Testament*, 2 vols., Sister Marie Aquinas McNamara, O.P. and Sister Maria Honoria Richter, O.P., trans., St. Louis: B. Herder, 1963, 1965.

—— "agape, love" in *idem.*, *Theological Lexicon of the New Testament*, James D. Ernest, trans., Peabody: Henrickson, 1994, 1:8–22.

Spieckermann, Hermann, "Mit der Liebe im Wort. Ein Beitrag zur Theologie des Deuteroniums" in Kratz and Spieckermann, 190–205.

Stapleton, Michael, *The Illustrated Dictionary of Greek and Roman Mythology*, New York: Peter Bedrick Books, 1986.

Stauffer, E., "ἀγαπάω, ἀγάπη, ἀγαπητός" [to love, love, beloved] in Gerhard Kittel, ed., Geoffrey W. Bromiley, trans. and ed., *Theological Dictionary of the New Testament*, Grand Rapids: Eerdmans, 1964, 1:21–55.

Ste. Croix, G. E. M. de, "Early Christian Attitudes to Property and Slavery" in Derek Baker, ed., *Church, Society and Politics*, Oxford: Blackwell, 1975, 1–38.

Stein, K. James, "Philipp Jakob Spener (1635–1705)" in Lindberg, ed., *The Pietist Theologians*, 84–99.

Stendhal, *On Love*, Philip Sidney Woolf and Cecil N. Sidney Woolf, trans., Mount Vernon, New York: The Peter Pauper Press, nd.

Stiegman, Emero, "Bernard of Clairvaux, William of St. Thierry, the Victorines" in Evans, *The Medieval Theologians*, 129–55.

Stock, Konrad, *Gottes wahre Liebe. Theologische Phänomenologie der Liebe*, Tübingen: Mohr Siebeck, 2000.

Stolt, Birgit, " 'Herzlich lieb habe ich dich, Herr, meine Stärke' (Ps.18,2)" in Oswald Bayer, Robert W. Jenson, and Simo Knuuttila, eds., *Caritas Dei. Beiträge zum Verständnis Luthers und der gegenwärtigen Ökumene. Festschrift für Tuomo Mannermaa zum 60. Geburtstag*, Helsinki: Luther-Agricola-Gesellschaft, 1997, 405–21.

Streiker, Lowell D., "The Christian Understanding of Platonic Love. A Critique of Anders Nygren's *Agape and Eros*," *The Christian Scholar* (1964), 331–40.

Tafferner, Andrea, *Gottes- und Nächstenliebe in der deutschsprachigen Theologie des 20. Jahrhunderts*, Innsbruck/Vienna: Tyrolia, 1992.

Taylor, Mark Kline, *Paul Tillich. Theologian of the Boundaries*, Minneapolis: Fortress Press, 1991.

Terry, Patricia, trans. and ed., *The Honeysuckle and the Hazel Tree. Medieval Stories of Men and Women*, Berkeley: University of California Press, 1995.

Tertullian, "Apology" in *The Ante-Nicene Fathers*, Vol. 3, Grand Rapids: Eerdmans, 1950–1957.

Theissen, Gerd, "Amor du Prochain et Égalité," *Etudes Théologiques & Religieuses* 76 (2001/3), 325–46.

Thornton, Bruce S., *Eros. The Myth of Ancient Greek Sexuality*, Boulder, CO/Oxford: Westview Press, 1997.

Thraede, Klaus, "Soziales Verhalten und Wohlfahrtspflege in der griechisch-römischen Antike (späte Republik und frühe

Kaiserzeit)'' in Gerhard Schäfer and Theodor Strohm, eds., *Diakonie – biblische Grundlagen und Orientierungen*, Heidelberg: Heidelberger Verlagsanstalt, 1990, 44–63.

Tillich, Paul, *Biblical Religion and the Search for Ultimate Reality*, Chicago: University of Chicago Press, 1955.

—— ''The Power of Love'' and ''Love is Stronger than Death'' in his *The New Being*, New York: Charles Scribner's Sons, 1955.

—— *Theology of Culture*, New York: Oxford University Press, 1959.

—— *Love, Power, and Justice*, New York: Oxford University Press, 1960.

—— *A History of Christian Thought from Its Judaic and Hellenistic Origins to Existentialism*, Carl E. Braaten, ed., New York: Simon and Schuster, 1967.

Uhlhorn, Gerhard, *Die christliche Liebestätigkeit*, 3 vols., Stuttgart, 1882–1890, repr. 1959.

Vacek, Edward Collins, S. J., *Love, Human and Divine: The Heart of Christian Ethics*, Washington, DC: Georgetown University Press, 1994.

Van Bavel, Tarsicius J., ''The Double Face of Love in St. Augustine: The Daring Inversion 'Love is God' '' *Atti del Congresso internazionale su S. Agostino nel XVI centenario della Conversione*, V. Grossi, ed., 3 vols., Rome: Institutum Patristicum Augustinianum, 1987, 3:69–80.

—— ''Love'' in Fitzgerald, ed., *Augustine through the Ages*, 509–16.

Vauchez, Andre, ed. in conjunction with Barrie Dobson and Michael Lapidge, *Encyclopedia of the Middle Ages*, 2 vols., Adrian Walford, trans., Chicago and London: Fitzroy Dearborn Publishers, 2000.

Völkl, Richard, *Frühchristliche Zeugnisse zu Wesen und Gestalt der christlichen Liebe*, Freiburg im Breisgau: Lambertus Verlag, 1963.

—— *Botschaft und Gebot der Liebe nach der Bibel*, Freiburg im Breisgau: Lambertus, 1964.

Wadell, Paul J., C. P., *The Primacy of Love. An Introduction to the Ethics of Thomas Aquinas*, New York: Paulist Press, 1992.

Wallmann, Johannes, "Johann Arndt (1555–1621)" in Lindberg, *The Pietist Theologians*, 21–37.

Weingart, Richard E., *The Logic of Divine Love. A Critical Analysis of the Soteriology of Peter Abailard*, Oxford: Clarendon Press, 1970.

Wengert, Timothy J., ed., *Harvesting Martin Luther's Reflections on Theology, Ethics, and the Church*, Grand Rapids: Eerdmans, 2004.

Whicher, George F., ed. and trans., *The Goliard Poets. Medieval Latin Songs and Satires*, New York: New Directions, 1965.

White, John Bradley, *A Study of the Language of Love in the Song of Songs and Ancient Egyptian Poetry*, Missoula: Scholars Press, 1978.

Wichern, Johann Hinrich, *Ausgewählte Schriften*, 3 vols., ed. by Karl Janssen, Gütersloh: Carl Bertelsmann Verlag, 1956–1962.

Wiesner-Hanks, Merry E., *Christianity and Sexuality in the Early Modern World: Regulating Desire, Reforming Practice*, London/ New York: Routledge, 2000.

Williams, Daniel Day, *The Spirit and Forms of Love*, New York: Harper & Row, 1968.

Wingren, Gustaf, *Theology in Conflict. Nygren, Barth, Bultmann*, E. Wahlstrom, trans., Philadelphia: Muhlenberg Press, 1958.

—— "Nygren, Anders (1890–1978)," *Theologische Realenzyklopädie*, Bd 24, 711–15.

Witte, John, Jr., *From Sacrament to Contract. Marriage, Religion and Law in the Western Tradition*, Louisville: Westminster John Knox Press, 1997.

—— and Robert M. Kingdon, *Sex, Marriage, and Family in John Calvin's Geneva*, Grand Rapids: Eerdmans, 2005.

Younger, John G., *Sex in the Ancient World from A to Z*, London/ New York: Routledge, 2005.

Index